WHATEVER BECAME OF . . . ?

Fifth Series

WHATEVER BECAME OF . . . ?

Fifth Series

by
Richard Lamparski

CROWN PUBLISHERS, INC., NEW YORK

Acknowledgments

The author would like to express thanks to the following people who helped in the preparation of this book: Michael Knowles (a colleague), Dick Lynch, Don Miller, Cinemabilia, Kirk Crivello, Marvin Paige, Charles Higham, Jon Virzi, Joe Riccuiti, Don Koll, Danny Frank, *Movie Star News*, George Eells, De Witt Bodeen, Curtis Harrington, Tony Slide, Wayne Clark, Jeanne Youngson, Leonard Maltin, *Film Fan Monthly*, Ene Riisna, Anselma Dell' Olio, Joseph O'Donohue IV, Malcolm Leo, Chris Albertson, Helen Bernstein, Burt Braff, Eric Barnouw, Tommy Cooper, Martitia Palmer, Jack Foster, John Scott Miller, Travis W. Armstrong, Bob Chatterton, and Eddie Brandt's Saturday Matinee.

Individuals whose names are footnoted (1, 2, 3, and 4) in the text appear as separate segments in previous volumes in this series. Footnote 1 refers to Volume One of *Whatever Became of . . . ?* , footnote 2 refers to *Whatever Became of . . . ? Second Series*, footnote 3 refers to *Whatever Became of . . . ? Third Series*, and footnote 4 refers to *Whatever Became of . . . ? Fourth Series*.

© 1974 by Richard Lamparski

First publication December, 1974

Printed in the United States of America
Published simultaneously in Canada by General Publishing Company Limited

Library of Congress Cataloging in Publication Data

Lamparski, Richard.
   Whatever became of . . . ?

   Includes index.
   1. United States—Biography.   2. Performing Arts—
United States—Biography.   I. Title.
CT220.L285   1975   790.2′092′2 [B]   72-96665
ISBN 0-517-51685-3

This book is for two friends:
My old one
ROBERT G. YOUNGSON
1917–1974
And my new one
BRITON ERWIN-KERR
1974–

CONTENTS

In Alphabetical Order

During the 1940s Gene Tierney was one of Twentieth Century-Fox's most prominent stars.

GENE TIERNEY

The movie beauty was born to wealthy parents in Brooklyn on November 20, 1920. She was educated in private schools in Connecticut and Switzerland.

After turning down a contract with Warner Brothers, Gene debuted on Broadway in *Mrs. O'Brien Entertains* (1938). She was with Columbia Pictures for a short time but left before they could put her into a film. After playing the ingenue in *The Male Animal* on Broadway she was pacted by M-G-M. When that studio couldn't find a property for her Twentieth Century-Fox signed her. She finally made her movie debut in *The Return of Frank James* (1940). The next year she registered in a showy part in *Tobacco Road*.

Many of her films were wrong for her. But even when the parts suited Gene she was never more than adequate. She was never really bad, however, and was always so pretty almost everyone forgave her lack of talent.

Her credits include: *Sundown* (1941), *Heaven Can Wait* (1943), *A Bell for Adano* (1945), *The Razor's Edge* (1946), *Close to My Heart* (1951), *Black Widow* (1954), and *Advise and Consent* (1962).

She was only twenty-one when she married the sophisticated fashion designer Oleg Cassini. During her first pregnancy Gene contracted German measles and gave birth to a retarded daughter. When her marriage came apart she entered into a well-publicized affair with the late Ali Kahn. Many felt their break-up was the last straw. She returned to the United States in 1955 and sought psychiatric help. The next the public heard Gene Tierney had committed herself to the Menninger Clinic.

An earlier relationship which left Gene despondent was revealed recently by Otto Preminger. According to the director, she would have become Mrs. John F. Kennedy if the future President's family had not disapproved of her as being "unsuitable."

Twice afterward studios signed her for comeback vehicles and twice she had to beg off at the last minute. Her last appearance before a camera was on an episode of *The F.B.I.* in 1970.

The picture that really put Gene Tierney over was *Laura* (1944), a role she got after Hedy Lamarr turned it down. In July of 1960, just as soon as his divorce from Miss Lamarr was final, Texas oilman Howard Lee and Gene were married.

Although she does not rule out acting again Gene seems to have found herself doing charity work. She is active raising funds for cancer research, mental health and the care of retarded children. For a while after moving to Houston she wrote a column in the local newspaper in which she reminisced about her Hollywood days. In a recent interview Gene spoke of her new life: "It's like being in a dark tunnel for so long you think it's endless and then suddenly you come out into the light."

Gene is now living in Houston and heavily engaged in charitable work. (Copyright 1974 *The Houston Post*)

Jack Benny had been on the air a year before Mary joined the cast of his program in 1933. *(NBC Photo)*

MARY LIVINGSTONE

The wise-cracking radio comedienne was born Sadie Marks in 1908.

Her father, the head of a synagogue in Vancouver, British Columbia, often invited Jewish performers to his home for Sabbath dinner. When the Marx Brothers were asked they brought along Jack Benny. Mary was only thirteen years old at the time and the comedian soon left with an aside to Zeppo Marx [4]: "Why did you bring me here with all these kids?" She felt so insulted that when she later went to see his vaudeville show with a group of friends Mary made them all promise not to laugh at anything he said.

Six years later Mary and Benny met on a group date in Los Angeles where her family had moved. Jack was paired off with another girl but the next day he called Mary for a date. They were married in New York City on January 14, 1927.

When the actress who played the dumb girl in Benny's act quit he asked Mary to fill in. She has said that she did it because "it was more interesting than sitting around hotel rooms." She had no career ambitions and wasn't a bit nervous. From the beginning she got laughs.

Benny had been on the air a year before Mary first appeared on his program in 1933. She debuted as "Mary Livingstone from Plainfield, New Jersey" and read a poem.

Her lilting giggle and skilled delivery of snide remarks went over very well on radio. Her quips were usually directed at Benny's thrift. Occasionally she was the brunt of Benny's jokes which usually were about her sister Babe or the fact that Mary had been selling hosiery at the May Company when she and Jack met the second time. Eventually the Bennys bought the Palm Springs home of the owner of the department store chain.

In 1958 she announced her retirement with an admission to what insiders long knew. As Mary's popularity had grown on radio so had her fears of the audience. "Sundays," she said, "became torturous for me."

The Bennys live in a large modern apartment in Beverly Hills. Mary, who was on the Best Dressed List several times during her career, still has a keen interest in fashion. She and Jack are grandparents by their one child, Joan, whom they adopted in 1936.

Mary Livingstone may still be missed by fans of the *Jack Benny Show*, but to many of the regulars and guests on that program she is remembered as a very difficult person to work with.

Mary Livingstone, Jonas Salk. (*Los Angeles* Times)

One of Wilding's first important films to be seen in the United States was the Alexander Korda production of *An Ideal Husband* in 1948.

MICHAEL WILDING

The English actor was born in Westcliff, Essex, England, on July 23, 1912. His father was a career army officer and his mother was a fairly well-known actress.

At first his talent seemed to lie in art. He was doing sketches for sets at the Elstree Studios when the acting bug bit. He began doing extra work and bit parts but quickly graduated to small roles as cads, policemen, butlers, and villains. It was when he played noblemen that he started to be noticed.

In 1935 he debuted in the West End in *Chase the Ace*. After scoring in *The Gate Revue* (1939) with Hermione Gingold, Michael got his first lead in the film *There Ain't No Justice* (1939). Some of his other English pictures were: *Convoy* (1941), *Kipps* (1942), *In Which We Serve* (1942), and *Stage Fright* (1950).

He came to Hollywood to make *The Law and the Lady* (1951) and was given an M-G-M contract.

On February 21, 1952, one year after he divorced the actress Kay Young, he married Elizabeth Taylor. Michael was over twice her age and described her at the time as "a mere child at heart."

Although he never became a star in the United States, Wilding was for a time quite active in pictures: *Torch Song* (1953), *The Egyptian* (1954), with Edmund Purdom (living in Rome), *The Scarlet Coat* (1955), *The World of Suzie Wong* (1960), and *The Best of Enemies* (1962).

Michael and Elizabeth Taylor were divorced in 1957 but have remained on very good terms. They are now grandparents by the oldest of their two children.

In 1963 he announced that he was giving up acting and joined a Hollywood talent agency which represented his ex-wife. When Miss Taylor left that office he was soon dropped from the payroll. The explanation at the time was that he was "hopeless about money."

In 1964 he married Margaret Leighton whom he had known since they made *Under Capricorn* (1949). They live quietly in a cottage they own in Chichester, Sussex.

In 1965 Wilding won an out-of-court settlement of six figures from the late Hedda Hopper. In her book *The Whole Truth and Nothing But* she had suggested that Michael and his close friend Stewart Granger were lovers.

One of his few professional appearances in the last ten years was as his wife's escort in a ballroom scene in *Lady Caroline Lamb* (1973). Miss Leighton played one of the leads while Wilding, who had once been among the top ten British film stars, didn't even have a line of dialogue.

Michael and his wife, Margaret Leighton, share a cottage in Chichester, Sussex, in England. *(John Timbers)*

Nils Asther was one of the most handsome men on the screen.

NILS ASTHER

The legendary figure of the screen was born on January 17, 1897, in Malmo, Sweden. He attended the University of Lundy and studied acting at Stockholm's Royal Dramatic School. Like Garbo he was considered a "discovery" of director Mauritz Stiller.

Asther's career like his personal life is full of contradictions and mysteries. He was brought to the United States to play in the silent Duncan Sisters starrer *Topsy and Eva* (1927). Three years later he eloped with Vivian Duncan.[3] It was his only marriage and produced a daughter, Evelyne. They were divorced after two years. But shortly after his debut he signed an M-G-M contract and made quite a splash in silents such as *The Cardboard Lover* (1928) with Jetta Goudal (married to Los Angeles decorator Howard Grieve), *Our Dancing Daughters* (1928), and *Wild Orchids* (1929). In the latter he was opposite Greta Garbo and rumors of their romance persisted for years.

His rich voice should have been a great boost to his career in talkies but the studios felt his European accent should be reserved for roles as heavies. He objected and although he managed to land romantic leads in pictures such as *The Sea Bat* (1930) with Racquel Torres (living in Malibu) and *Storm at Daybreak* (1933), they were not box-office successes. He received very good notices for his portrayal of the title role in *The Bitter Tea of General Yen* (1933). In it however he was costumed and heavily made-up. This only strengthened the thinking that he was too exotic looking and sounding.

He made *Letty Lynton* (1932), *The Right to Romance* (1933) with Ann Harding (living in Westport, Connecticut), and *Madame Spy* (1934), and

14

then went to England for five years. His British movies did nothing to further his career. Some were: *Abdul the Damned* (1935) with Patric Knowles (living in Los Angeles) and *Guilty Melody* (1937). He returned to mostly programmers like *Dr. Kildaire's Wedding Day* (1941) in which he was billed tenth, *Sweater Girl* (1942) with Johnny Johnson (now a manufacturer of golf carts and living in Phoenix, Arizona), and *Jealousy* (1945) with the late Hugo Haas. He was billed seventh in *The Feathered Serpent* (1948) with the late Mantan Moreland.[3] Two noteworthy pictures he made during those years were *The Night of January 16th* (1941) with Ellen Drew (Mrs. James Herbert of Palm Desert, California) and *The Man in Half Moon Street* (1944). In the latter he was very effective and still extremely handsome.

Throughout the fifties there were persistent rumors that he was loading trucks at $1.00 an hour and sorting mail at the Los Angeles post office. In 1959 he was interviewed as he left the country for the last time. He complained bitterly about the stories printed about him and denied them all. One which still persists is that Greta Garbo stepped into an elevator, found that he was the operator, and fainted. His reply was that he had neither seen nor heard from her in over thirty years.

The man who was once paid $5,000 a week to be with Pola Negri[1] in *The Loves of an Actress* (1928) still acts occasionally in both Copenhagen and Stockholm. He has also developed quite a talent for painting. Asther lives alone in a small ultra-modern apartment community in the suburbs of Stockholm. It is in a wooded area and was the first such structure in the world to be lighted and heated by atomic power.

Nils lives in an atomically heated apartment complex outside Stockholm. (*Jon Virzi*)

Marion was on Arthur Godfrey's television and radio shows for five years in the 1950s.

MARION MARLOWE

The popular soprano from television of the 1950s was born Marion Townsend in St. Louis on March 7, 1929. She began taking vocal lessons when she was twelve years old and later studied at London's Royal Conservatory under Sir Thomas Beecham. She roomed with Marilyn Monroe at Hollywood's Studio Club while being coached by Sigmund Romberg.

When Arthur Godfrey found Marion on January 9, 1951, she was singing at Miami's Kenilworth Hotel for $35.00 a night. She had never heard of him and refused to take his offer seriously. After he gave her a $100 advance she consented to come to New York for one appearance on his television show.

From the beginning she was a favorite with audiences of his Wednesday night TV show and morning television and radio program.

Publicity made Marion and Frank Parker a hot item when actually their exchange of longing glances during duets was nothing more than showmanship. Her real romance was with Godfrey's producer Larry Puck. Dating among Godfrey employees was frowned upon, however. Julius La Rosa had been fired when he dated a McGuire sister. When Marion received her engagement ring from Puck Godfrey asked her to show it on camera. Two days later he fired her. She has never seen him since that day.

16

Frank Parker and Marion have dinner together occasionally. He is completely retired and living in Manhattan. Most of his time is spent painting. Now and then she runs into Julius La Rosa who is a New York City disc jockey and Jeanette Davis, a housewife and mother living in Syosset, New York. Lu Ann Sims (a Godfrey vocalist) lives in Reseda, California.

Marion went straight from her five and one half year Godfrey stint into an exclusive contract with Ed Sullivan. She was immediately booked into all the leading nightclubs in the country. Everyone wanted to see the girl who had been so abruptly fired and her price quadrupled.

In 1959 she was on Broadway in *The Sound of Music* and she replaced Joan Diener in the ANTA production of *Man of La Mancha*. During those years and now when she plays dinner theatres people still ask about her days with Godfrey. "They want to know if it really was one big happy family," she says. "Yes, it was like that until Julius was fired. After that no one trusted anyone again."

Marion is a widow and lives in Sea Bright, New Jersey. "I have a very nice life today," she told an interviewer. "But my values are nearly all changed. I spent years looking for the wrong things in the wrong places." Her chief interests now are the stray animals she takes in, her organic garden, and metaphysics.

Richard Lamparski and Marion after a recent interview. *(Toni Lopopolo)*

Jimmy and friends during a Texaco commercial telecast on February 28, 1952.

JIMMY NELSON

The television ventriloquist was born in Chicago on December 15, 1928. A former vaudevillian turned policeman encouraged Jimmy's early interest in performing. He would tell the youngster stories about the headliners he had worked with during the 1920s. But it was the *Chase and Sanborn Hour* that inspired him to become a ventriloquist. The popular radio show was heard Sunday nights and starred Edgar Bergen,[2] an old alumnus from Jimmy's Lake View high school. The two didn't meet until the 1950s when Jimmy was playing the Mapes Hotel in Reno—hospitalized with appendicitis, Jimmy's idol flew in and subbed for him. "It was the greatest thrill of my professional life," says Jimmy today.

Jimmy's first and most famous dummy, Danny O'Day (he describes him as a "blasphemous piece of balsam"), was carved by the same artist who created Charlie McCarthy years before.

While still in school Jimmy appeared in neighborhood theatres and small clubs. Upon graduation he toured the Midwest. It was the night-club boom of post World War II America. Most of his bookings were in such towns as Carbondale, Illinois, or Evanston, Indiana, but they gave him the training and experience he needed.

As early as 1949 he had his own TV show in Chicago, but when he was booked into the Radio City Music Hall in 1951 Jimmy thought he had really hit the big time.

In the meanwhile, Sid Stone, who had become famous on Milton Berle's TV show as the pitchman (he coined the phrase "Tell ya' what I'm gonna' do"), was leaving, and the producers were looking for a ventriloquist. Señor Wences was auditioned but found unsuitable because of his heavy accent. Someone caught Nelson's act and he was offered a contract to appear as a regular on the enormously popular *Texaco Star*

Theatre, the Berle show. The hitch was that they wanted him to do the commercial. At the time, it was considered beneath the dignity of most performers, and Jimmy's agent warned him against accepting. But beginning New Year's Day, 1952, Jimmy and Danny began their two-year stint doing their act plus a five-minute commercial smack in the middle of the show. Every Tuesday night 40 million people saw them, and overnight they were household names.

During the 1954 and 1955 seasons they were seen on their own ABC show, *Come Closer,* and it was at this time that Jimmy began his ten-year association with Nestles as their TV spokesman (he was constantly interrupted by Farfel, the sad-eyed erudite dog dummy, with his nasal pronunciation of "chaw-clit"). Throughout the 1950s Nelson, with Danny, Farfel, and Fa-ta-ta-tee-ta, the cat dummy, was a frequent guest on TV variety shows such as Ed Sullivan's. As late as 1963–64, Jimmy and company were featured on *Studio 99½* over Channel 13 in New York City.

For the past decade, Nelson, who resides in Cape Coral, Florida, with his wife and six children, has done very well, appearing at fairs around the country as well as at many industrial shows.

The Danny dummies sell even better today than when they were introduced nearly twenty years ago, and Jimmy has put out two LPs on how to become a ventriloquist. He is preparing a third LP featuring his daughter Marianne, who has become quite skilled at the art and is her dad's most severe critic. His newest character is Humphrey Higsbye, a horn-rimmed, pompous misfit.

Of his talent, Jimmy says that it is impossible to throw one's voice. "It's a trick by which the audience's attention is diverted from me to a dummy. People know it's me talking but they want to be fooled. If I said the same things Danny or Farfel say, I'd fall on my face. I've tried it alone and I'm absolutely lost on stage by myself."

Jimmy stands behind Danny O'Day, Farfel, and his new dummy Humphrey Higsbye. *(Michael Knowles)*

In 1937 *Ring* magazine picked Henry
as the Fighter of the Year.

HENRY ARMSTRONG

The only boxer to hold three World Championships at the same time
was born one of sixteen children on December 12, 1912, in Columbus,
Mississippi. His real name is Henry Jackson. During the early part of
his ring career he fought under the name "Melody" Jackson. Later he took
the name Armstrong because there was another fighter named Jackson.
Armstrong originally intended to become a long-distance runner but went
into boxing as an amateur in 1929 when he learned that he could earn
large amounts of money.

After winning 58 out of his 62 amateur bouts Henry turned professional
in 1932. He had been eliminated from the Olympics that year in San
Francisco. He won 8 decisions and KO'd 5 in 1932. In 1933 he won 8, 5 by
knock-outs, and lost 1. Next year he was the victor against 7 opponents
and was beaten by 2. In 1935 he won 5 of his 7 contests. The following
year he lost 3 but KO'd 6 and took the decision on another 5. Then on
October 29, 1937, in Madison Square Garden he knocked out Petey
Sarron in the sixth round and became Featherweight Champion of the
World. On May 31, 1938, Henry won a decision and unseated the late
Barney Ross in Long Island City, thus taking the Welterweight crown.
His high point was reached on August 17, 1938, when he outpointed
Lou Ambers in Madison Square Garden for the Lightweight Champion-
ship. Ambers took his title back on August 22, 1939, but for one year
and five days Henry Armstrong did what no man before or since has ever

done—he was Featherweight, Welterweight, and Lightweight Champion of the World simultaneously.

He relinquished the Featherweight title in late 1938 when he could not make the weight. In 1940 he became the contender for the Middleweight crown but Ceferino Garcia retained it on March 1. Many still feel that Henry won that fight but the judges gave the decision to Garcia. Fritzie Zivic took Henry's Welterweight title away from him on October 4, 1940. They were rematched the following January and this time Zivic knocked Armstrong out in the twelfth round.

He had been chosen *Ring* magazine's Fighter of the Year in 1937 and in 1940 was awarded the Edward J. Neil Trophy. In 1954 he made the Boxing Hall of Fame.

In 1940 he starred in the all-black feature *Keep Punching*.

Armstrong fought on until his retirement in 1945. One of the 10 men he KO'd in 1942 was Zivic who by then had lost his crown. Henry took 10 of his 13 matches in 1943 and KO'd 10 opponents the following year.

After hanging up his gloves professionally he toured in an all-sports unit of an entertainment program for U.S. troops all over the world.

When he was a child his mother, who was half Cherokee Indian, predicted repeatedly that Henry would first do something very unique and then would spend the second half of his life as a preacher. He is now Reverend Jackson who travels to Baptist churches throughout the country on weekends. Monday through Friday he is assistant director of the Boys' Club of St. Louis.

The man who was dubbed "Perpetual Motion" and "Hurricane" Jackson because of his aggressiveness and tenacity made as much as $80,000 a fight but was surprised to find how little money he had when he quit.

Is he tired of people asking him why he left the ring for the pulpit? "Not a bit," he says. "That's when I get the chance to tell them what I found in Jesus."

The former World's Champion is now Rev. Henry Armstrong living in St. Louis, Missouri. *(Michael Knowles)*

Moments after being crowned Miss America in Atlantic City in September of 1943.

MISS AMERICA OF 1943

Jean Bartel, the first co-ed to win the coveted title, was born Jean Bartelmeh on October 26, in Los Angeles. As early as she can remember her ambition was to be on Broadway. When she was fourteen years old she dropped the last syllable of her surname, lied about her age, and joined a local production of *The Desert Song*. Her fellow choristers were the then unknowns Jerome Hines and John Raitt.

Jean entered the Miss California contest reluctantly and even after taking that title a friend had to convince her that the Atlantic City pageant was more than a leg show before she would go. She sang "Night and Day" for the judges, who also took into consideration her dimensions: bust—34.1, waist—24.2, hips—35.0.

After winning she turned down an offer of $1,500 a week to appear at the Roxy Theatre in favor of a 40-city, 24-state tour at the height of World War II before audiences in hospitals, war industries, armed service bases, and at bond rallies.

Jean received a citation from the Treasury Department for selling more Series E bonds than anyone else that year—$2,500,000 worth. One man bought $50,000 worth from her. Another took a $5,000 bond in exchange for the pair of hose she was wearing. Almost forty years later, Lenora

Slaughter, who is to the Miss America Pageant what Avery Brundage is to the Olympics, described Jean's reign in the book *There She Is:* "Every succeeding Miss America owes her the greatest debt. She was a smash hit all around." Jean is further credited with being the first title holder to whom women really responded. Eighty percent of the bonds she sold were to women.

While Jean has served as a judge in the years since and speaks well of her experience she also admits that the most she realized during her year as Miss America was a paltry $3,000 and that she subsisted during much of the tour on a diet of milk and chocolate bars. The following year she had to pay her own way back to Atlantic City to relinquish her crown.

She realized her great ambition when she played the female lead in the revival of *Of Thee I Sing* on Broadway in 1952. She has hosted her own TV series *It's a Woman's World* and *Focus on Women*. In 1949 she helped the C.I.A. to apprehend a Nazi operating out of Lebanon under the guise of an impressario. She was the first TV journalist to interview Sweden's Princess Christina in the Royal Palace in Stockholm, and she produced and narrated *The 5 Faces of Madame Ky* for NET.

Jean was married for the first time in 1970 to William J. Hogue, the vice-president of a conglomerate. The couple share the same Westwood, California, home in which she grew up. Now a TV consultant, she said recently of her marriage and career: "All of my wants have been fulfilled."

The former Miss America is a Christian Scientist.

She's now a Mrs. and lives in West Los Angeles, California. *(Shelly Brodsky)*

Ruth in her costume for the *Ziegfeld Follies of 1931. (NBC Radio)*

RUTH ETTING

The superstar songstress of the 1920s and 1930s was born on November 23, 1897, in David City, Nebraska, and brought up on her grandfather's farm. After graduating from high school she enrolled at Chicago's Academy of Fine Arts.

When Ruth found mathematics too difficult she switched from architecture, her original major, to costume design. She was sent to the Marigold Gardens to do sketches for the nightclub's costumer. When the male singer was unable to go on one night Ruth substituted although the only time she had ever sung publicly was in a church choir. Her unusual voice, called at the time "female baritone," caused a mild sensation in Chicago. One of her first enthusiasts was a small-time underworld character named Moe "The Gimp" Snyder.

Irving Berlin brought Ruth to the attention of Florenz Ziegfeld, who signed her for his *Follies of 1927.* She was with him for five years in *Whoopee* (1928), *Simple Simon* (1930), and *Ziegfeld Follies of 1931.*

Snyder and Ruth were married in 1922. He took complete charge of her career and her salary went from $25 a week to $2,500. But his bargaining methods, which were highly questionable, and his rude manner got him barred from the very clubs, theatres, and radio stations where she sang.

24

Their Svengali-Trilby relationship ended on October 15, 1938, when "The Gimp" shot Ruth's pianist Myrl Alderman. Snyder got a year in prison for his act and is now working for Mayor Daley in Chicago's City Hall. Ruth and Alderman were married two months after the shooting.

The Aldermans were hurt and embarrassed by the bad press from the shooting and Snyder's trial. Then Alderman's ex-wife brought an unsuccessful alienation of affection suit. They withdrew to Colorado Springs, Colorado, where Ruth still lives. Alderman died in 1966.

Contrary to rumor Ruth Etting is far from a recluse. She travels, kept in touch with Blossom Seeley[4] until her recent death, is still close with George Burns, and corresponds with fans all over the world.

Biograph recently put out *Hello Baby,* a recording of some of her old hits: "Glad Rag Doll," "Ain't Misbehavin'," and "You're the Cream in My Coffee." She is particularly happy to hear from young people who are just discovering her through the album. Although her renditions of "At Sundown," "It All Depends on You," and "Shine on Harvest Moon" sold in the millions and earned her the title "Sweetheart of Columbia Records," she has never until *Hello Baby* received a penny in royalties.

Ruth was not happy with the 1955 filmusical of her life *Love Me or Leave Me.* "It was half fairy tale," Miss Etting told an interviewer recently. "It's a shame that the most beautiful part of my life, my twenty-eight-year marriage to Myrl Alderman, was left out completely because that was the real highlight of my life story."

Ruth lives now in Colorado Springs, Colorado.

In the early 1930s Frances was under contract to Paramount Pictures.

FRANCES DEE

The beautiful leading lady of the screen was born Jean Dee in Pasadena, California, on November 27, 1907. Her father, an army officer, moved his family to Chicago where Frances grew up and where she attended the University of Chicago. In 1929 he was reassigned to Los Angeles.

Frances caught the movie bug and landed a job as an extra in the Lois Moran (the widow of the president of American Airlines lives now in Sedona, Arizona) starrer *Words and Music* (1929). Shortly afterward she entered a contest held by Paramount to publicize one of their college movies. She was called to the studio on an interview and was lunching in the commissary when Maurice Chevalier spotted her. Within days she was signed to play the love interest in his vehicle *Playboy of Paris* (1930).

Frances was never starred in her pictures but she played opposite some of the top male stars of the day: Phillips Holmes in *An American Tragedy* (1931), Buddy Rogers [3] in *This Reckless Age* (1932), Gary Cooper in *Souls at Sea* (1937), Ronald Colman in *If I Were King* (1938), John Wayne in *A Man Betrayed* (1941), and William Holden in *Meet the Stewarts* (1942).

She was also in *King of the Jungle* (1933), Hollywood's first all-color feature *Becky Sharp* (1935), *I Walked with a Zombie* (1943), *Patrick the Great* (1945) with Peggy Ryan (living in Honolulu), and *The Private Affairs of Bel Ami* (1947).

She was also Meg in the memorable *Little Women* (1933).

In 1933 Frances married Joel McCrea.[3] The following year they had their first boy. He acts occasionally under the name Jody McCrea. Their second son was born in 1935 and now manages one of the McCrea's several ranches. Twenty years later Frances bore another son.

Frances and Joel made a number of films together. Among them were: *The Silver Cord* (1933) with Irene Dunne,[1] *Wells Fargo* (1937), and *Four Faces West* (1948).

As early as 1935 the McCreas separated but were soon reconciled. In 1966 it was her husband who filed for divorce charging Frances with cruelty. They are still married however and living together at their various homes in California. The McCreas are millionaires several times over from their investments in real estate.

She announced her retirement from the screen several times but continued making pictures until *Gypsy Colt* in 1954.

Occasionally she and her husband are seen at Hollywood premieres and functions honoring one of their contemporaries. Frances avoids interviews. Her main interest is in the Moral Re-Armament movement.

Joel McCrea and Frances Dee are seen frequently at Hollywood movie premieres. *(Jon Virzi)*

By 1954 Philbrick's testimony had sent 11 Communists to prison, his book was a best seller and had been made into a popular TV series. The former counterspy was then running a general store in Rye, New York. *(U.P.I.)*

HERBERT A. PHILBRICK

The double agent who became a household word at the height of the Cold War was born on May 11, 1915, and raised in New England.

In 1940 Philbrick's job as an advertising salesman brought him in contact with the Massachusetts Youth Council. The organization's expressed purpose was anti-war activities. He felt in sympathy with their goals and was soon in charge of the movement's Cambridge operation. When Philbrick discovered that the literature he was distributing was similar to that of the Communist Party he went to the F.B.I.

From that day on he was an undercover agent. In February 1944 he joined the Communist Party, all the time reporting everything he heard and observed to the F.B.I.

It was not until April 6, 1949, that he blew his cover. Eleven high-ranking U.S. Communists were on trial in federal court charged with violation of the Smith Act. Philbrick's surprise appearance as a prosecution witness was dramatic and decisive. They were all found guilty.

Overnight Philbrick was a national hero to many Americans. In *I Led Three Lives* which was a 1952 best seller he described the triple life he led for nine years as "a citizen, a Communist, and a counterspy." A TV series starring Richard Carlson (now a writer living in Sherman Oaks) as *Comrade Herb* was shown on U.S. screens for several seasons and lasted over ten years in syndication.

Although his fame with the general public has faded, Philbrick still enjoys a good income from his lectures and the weekly newsletter which he provides for right-wing publications.

His fourth life is being spent with his second wife who is over twenty years his junior. She once worked for his friend Dr. Fred Schwarz (the Australian physician who toured the United States in the early sixties with his Christian Anti-Communist Crusade, which is now centered in Long Beach, California).

The Philbricks feel their lives are still in danger and use aliases for almost everything. They would like to return to New England but feel safer in Bethesda, Maryland, where their home is only minutes away from the headquarters of the C.I.A. Most of their neighbors work for either the C.I.A. or the F.B.I.

A few years ago *The New York Times* revealed that most of *I Led Three Lives* was ghost-written by Fendall Yerza. The author was quoted as describing Philbrick as "quite naive, socially and politically."

Philbrick is still a popular lecturer among right-wing groups. *(U.P.I.)*

Allan was loaned to Universal by his studio to make *Show Boat* in 1936.

ALLAN JONES

The singing star of the movies was born in Old Forge, Pennsylvania, on October 14, 1908. His Welsh-born father was a mine foreman with a passionate love of music. Allan soloed as a boy soprano in his church choir when he was eight years old.

He worked in and around coal mines from the age of eleven until he graduated from high school. With the $1,500 he had saved Jones studied at the Music School of the University of Syracuse and then in Paris.

After returning to the United States Allan toured in musicals for the Shuberts. He was playing opposite Maria Jeritza[2] in *Annina* (1934) when M-G-M tested him for the lead in *Naughty Marietta*. The studio wanted him but the Shuberts asked $50,000 for his contract. By the time he was able to raise the money the picture had begun with Nelson Eddy in the part. It was an unfortunate beginning that Jones was never able to overcome. He said recently that he "always felt like I was being treated as a second fiddle after that."

His fine voice was put to good use in *Rose Marie* (1936), *The Firefly* (1937), and *The Great Victor Herbert* (1939). But his movie career never really caught fire. When he refused to use a broad Italian accent in *Everybody Sing* (1938) he was suspended. In the end he had his way but the studio punished him by not putting him in another film for a year. When he was finally free of his Metro contract M-G-M executive Eddie Mannix, with whom Jones had quarreled, made every attempt to have him taken off *The Fleischmann Hour,* a popular radio program.

He eventually was signed by Paramount for two pictures a year after Mannix tried his best to squash the deal.

Some of Allan's other pictures were: *A Night at the Opera* (1935), *A Day at the Races* (1937), *Honeymoon in Bali* (1939) with Osa Massen (single and living in Beverly Hills), *The Boys from Syracuse* (1940), and *When Johnny Comes Marching Home* (1942).

Although he never encouraged his son Jack Jones to perform, it was in Allan's nightclub act that he made his debut. His father is the only vocal coach Jack ever had. His other son is the editor of *Yachting* magazine. His one daughter is a songwriter. The mother of his children is Irene Hervey (living in Los Angeles) who divorced Jones in 1954.

Jones was retired during his marriage to Mary Florsheim, heiress to the shoe fortune. They were divorced in 1964. Since then he has toured in a number of shows such as *Man of La Mancha, The Fantasticks,* and *Guys and Dolls.*

Jones lives in a Manhattan high-rise apartment with his Cuban-born wife who is many years his junior.

The song most closely associated with Allan Jones is "The Donkey Serenade" which he often sings at curtain calls. It was also the personal favorite of its composer Rudolph Friml.[3] When he died in 1972 Jones, at Friml's request, sang it over his open grave.

Allan and his wife share a Manhattan apartment. *(Sheron Harkavy)*

In 1951 Hillary made *Lullaby of Broadway* for Columbia Pictures.

HILLARY BROOKE

The comedienne and "other woman" of movies was born Beatrice Sofia Mathilda Peterson on September 8, 1914, in Astoria, Long Island. Her older brother introduced her to John Powers, who suggested she model. She was the perfect type for the hats, squared shoulders, and suits of the period and did very well.

From modeling she got a chance to do *Set to Music* (1939) on Broadway with Bea Lillie (living on East End Avenue in Manhattan) and then went to London where she played in *Transatlantic Rhythm* (1936). Hollywood brought her out to be one of the *New Faces of 1937* but she wasn't happy with the picture and when no further offers were forthcoming she returned to New York. Former star Sue Carol was by now active as an agent and brought her back for a Paramount contract. She debuted in *Eternally Yours* (1939).

The studio considered her too intelligent and self-possessed to be sexy and the die of her movie career was cast. Then too she had neither the knack nor inclination toward studio politics and gravitated to people whom she found amusing. Although she never got the lead and seldom got the man Hillary turned up in some important pictures and her work in them holds up beautifully. A few were: *And the Angels Sing* (1944), *Ministry of Fear* (1944), *The Enchanted Cottage* (1945), *Never Wave at a WAC* (1953), and *The Man Who Knew Too Much* (1956).

Although she swears she never had any special training many fans believed she was British because of her flawless diction. Even the British magazine *Picturegoer* used to refer to her as "England's own."

Her good disposition and skill at comedy brought her featured roles opposite the top comics of the day, such as Bing Crosby and Bob Hope who had her in their *The Road to Utopia* (1945). Hope used her again in *Monsieur Beaucaire* (1946), and Red Skelton had her with him in *The Fuller Brush Man* (1948). She was also Lorelie Kilbourne in four *Big Town* features made in the late forties.

Although Hillary retired completely when she married M-G-M General Manager Ray Klune in 1960, she is very popular still, particularly among younger TV viewers. The *My Little Margie* series on which she played Charles Farrell's [2] girl friend is still in re-runs, and Abbott and Costello fans beg her for anecdotes about the pair. She was with them in their features *Africa Screams* (1949) and *Abbott and Costello Meet Captain Kidd* (1952) and worked frequently on their TV series. She stayed in touch with Bud Abbott [2] until his recent death.

"I loved making pictures and my experiences with Abbott and Costello hold wonderful, fun-filled memories for me but I don't want to work anymore," Hillary allowed during a recent interview. "I have the time and money to travel a great deal and when we are home I love to cook and go deep sea fishing."

Hillary's son by a previous marriage is an assistant movie director. The Klunes live in a modern condominium which overlooks a private race track in San Luis Rey Downs, California.

Hillary and her poodle Barney in the den of her home. *(Coleen Magee)*

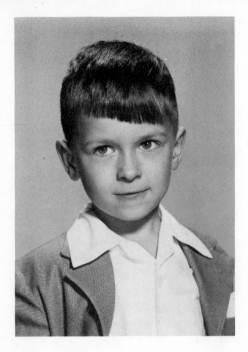

George's voice was only part of his charm.

GEORGE "FOGHORN" WINSLOW

The child actor with the basso profundo voice was born George Wenzlaff on May 3, 1946, in Los Angeles. His first "da da" was uttered in a startlingly deep baritone. He returned from his first Halloween disappointed because, in spite of his mask, all the neighbors knew who he was as soon as he spoke.

At the urging of his uncle, George's mother took him to audition for Art Linkletter's show. He came on wearing a trainman's outfit. When Linkletter asked his name he replied: "It's George but I'd rather be Casey Jones." The audience howled. The program had a strict rule that no child ever appeared more than once. George was brought back about twenty times on Linkletter's radio and TV shows.

Cary Grant caught one of the shows and signed George for his film *Room for One More* (1952) with Betsy Drake (living in Los Angeles where she teaches and writes). Warners put him under contract which Twentieth Century-Fox bought in 1953.

He appeared several times on *Blondie* and *Ozzie and Harriet* TV series and made in all 11 movies. But his distinctive voice and delightful attitude made an indelible impression on fans. Along with sounding funny, "Foghorn" had a humor all his own and he was totally unimpressed by the stars he worked with. When the waspish Clifton Webb made the mistake of being sarcastic with him during the filming of *Mister Scoutmaster* (1953), George topped every one of his lines to the delight of the crew and other players.

He played Marilyn Monroe's wealthy admirer in *Gentlemen Prefer Blondes* (1953). The scene in which he informs her that she has a "certain animal magnetism" is a classic.

His other pictures were *The Rocket Man* (1954), *Artists and Models* (1955), *Rock, Pretty Baby* (1957), and his last, *Wild Heritage* (1958). His one and only appearance before a camera since then was when he attempted an introduction for the TV premiere of *Mister Scoutmaster* in 1962. He was so awkward it was never used.

George seldom speaks of his career. The two boys he rooms with in Huntington Beach, California, didn't learn he had been in pictures until recently. They were his shipmates during the four years he spent in the Navy.

The money he earned as an actor was used "learning to play pinochle." He is currently taking a photography course at Orange Coast College. The deep voice that made him famous is completely gone.

He is most frequently asked about Marilyn Monroe. Says George: "The thing I remember most is working with this beautiful lady from early in the morning until late at night. Then as my folks were getting me dressed to go home she came out of her dressing room without any make-up. If I hadn't recognized her voice I'd never have believed she was the same person."

George is studying photography in college. *(Michael Harkavy)*

Gloria was named one of the Wampus Baby Stars of 1932.

GLORIA STUART

The blonde lovely of the talkies was born on the Fourth of July in Santa Monica, California. While majoring in philosophy at the University of California she wrote for the student newspaper and appeared in some plays at the Berkeley Playhouse. After graduation she spent some time in the artists' colony in Carmel-by-the-Sea doing more plays and working for the local newspaper.

Gloria was playing in *Twelfth Night* at the Pasadena Playhouse when Paramount and Universal studios became interested in her simultaneously. The matter was finally submitted to the Academy of Motion Picture Arts and Sciences to decide which company she would sign with. A flip of a coin put her under contract to Universal.

She made her debut on loan-out to Warner Brothers for the Kay Francis starrer *Street of Women* (1932). The same year she was chosen a Wampas Baby Star.

She was in the original *The Invisible Man* (1933), *Love Captive* (1934), *Laddie* (1935) with Grady Sutton (single and living in Hollywood), *Girl Overboard* (1937) with the late Sidney Blackmer, *Keep Smiling* (1938) with Robert Allen (living in Center Island, New York), and *The Three Musketeers* (1939).

In the few A pictures she made Gloria merely supported their stars. She is however very well remembered. As late as 1973 filmologist Don Miller wrote: "She was extremely attractive and graced every film she was in." Her pictures that play often on the Late Show and at film festivals are:

The Old Dark House (1932), *Roman Scandals* (1933), *Gold Diggers of 1935*, and *The Prisoner of Shark Island* (1936). She was in two Shirley Temple vehicles: *Poor Little Rich Girl* (1936) and *Rebecca of Sunnybrook Farm* (1938).

In 1934 Gloria divorced sculptor Blair Gordon Newell and married scenarist Arthur Sheekman who had co-authored some of Eddie Cantor's movies. As their family grew she began to lose interest in her career and by the forties she was making only a few films: *Here Comes Elmer* (1943), *The Whistler* (1944), *Enemy of Women* (1944) with Sigrid Gurie (living in Hollywood), and her last, *She Wrote the Book* (1946).

The Sheekmans travel extensively. After a 1954 tour of the art galleries in Paris Gloria returned to West Los Angeles and decided to paint. The results brought some very good notices when Manhattan's prestigious Hammer Galleries gave her a one-woman show in 1961.

She is friendly but quite firm in her refusal to be queried about her career. Recently she told a would-be interviewer: "I really think film buffs remember me and my pictures better than I do. I suppose I should be flattered but my interests today are elsewhere. Please understand, I am grateful for my Hollywood years and all the good things they gave me—my wonderful husband and our good friends."

Gloria Stuart, who is a grandmother, continues to travel and paint. She does portraits, primitives, and scenics.

Gloria today is an accomplished artist. *(Jon Virzi)*

Within a month of its release in 1962 *The First Family* album sold over 2,500,000 copies. *(U.P.I.)*

VAUGHN MEADER

The comedian who was hurtled from a $22,500-a-week career to instant oblivion when John F. Kennedy was assassinated was born Abbott Vaughn Meader in Boston in 1936.

Meader's father was killed when he was eighteen months old and his mother placed him in a series of children's homes while she supported herself as a waitress. Two women who ran the Parker Homestead School taught Vaughn to sing and play music.

He went out on his own in his early teens. Before attempting comedy he played with a country-western band in New England. He joined the army and spent several years in Germany where he met and married his first wife, Vera.

In 1959 the Meaders returned to the United States and while Vaughn made the rounds of agents' offices and auditions his wife worked to support them. Finally he got a job doing his routines in a Greenwich Village nightclub. From that he was invited on *Arthur Godfrey's Talent Scouts* TV show.

As John F. Kennedy was taking office Meader was polishing his imitation of him. It began as part of his stand-up comedy act. Within a year Meader had let his hair grow and even began to look like the President.

On November 7, 1962, his album of Kennedy impersonations, *The First Family,* was released. Within a month it had sold 2,500,000 copies. He was one of the highest paid and hottest entertainment personalities in the nation.

Then on November 22, 1963, JFK was killed. No performer ever became a has-been as quickly as Vaughn. His nightclub bookings were immediately cancelled as was the TV special he had just signed for. *The First Family* albums were returned to the manufacturer. His Kennedy impersonation was only part of his act but says Meader, "Nobody wanted to know from me. I was as dead as the President."

He has made several unsuccessful attempts at a comeback. His 1971 album *Whatever Happened to Vaughn Meader* didn't sell. His next, *The Second Coming,* on which he played Jesus Christ did much better but it didn't reestablish him.

Of the years in between Meader says: "I didn't identify with JFK like a lot of people thought. I never met him. It wasn't until Bobby was killed that the full impact hit me. I had a serious drinking problem. I lived in windowless shacks in the woods and in other people's basements. It was through LSD that I found peace. It was spiritual medicine for me but I no longer use it."

Today Meader has a new wife, many years his junior. He worked briefly as a $150 a week counselor at a drug rehabilitation center in Louisville, Kentucky. Currently he is planning to play JFK again in an off-Broadway presentation. He impersonated the late Walter Winchell in the current film *Lepke.*

Vaughn had rebelled against the Christianity that was drummed into him as a boy but now feels differently. Says the former humorist, "Jesus is the only sense I've been able to make out of this confused world. I'm a Jesus freak."

Vaughn Meader and his second wife Susan. *(Richard Schaeffer)*

Jane with Judy Clark wearing the pompadour hairstyle that was so popular in the 1940s.

JANE FRAZEE

The star of B musicals was born Mary Jane Freshe on July 18, 1918, in Duluth, Minnesota. Jane was only six years old when she and her sister Ruth began singing and dancing at businessmen's luncheons for $10 a performance.

They were in their early teens when the pair toured for eight months with a small revue. Their food budget during that period was $1.00 a day. In 1934 the Frazees landed in New York City. In a very short time the girls went from vaudeville to working in some very smart nightclubs. They were also featured as vocalists on a radio show with Larry Clinton and his Band sponsored by Sensation Cigarettes (10 cents a pack).

In 1939 they came to Hollywood where they were booked into the famous Clover Club, an illegal gambling operation on the Sunset Strip which paid top money. They were on the bill with the late Joe E. Lewis when it was raided.

The sisters were tested by several studios and made a number of shorts but Ruth did not register on film. Jane turned down a stock contract at M-G-M in favor of costarring with Johnny Downs [4] in the Republic feature *Melody Ranch* (1940). Then she was signed by Universal to a contract which began at $250 a week. She made mostly low-budget musicals. Their plots were often corny but they were unpretentious and were consistent money makers. The songs she was given to sing were seldom good ones and she was neither glamorous nor gorgeous. But Jane Frazee had a very real quality to her and she came over as very likeable.

Although she only made one A picture, *Practically Yours* (1944), she appeared in some features that are still popular on TV: *Buck Privates*

(1941) with Abbott and Costello, *Hellzapoppin* (1941), and *Beautiful But Broke* (1944). Some of her others were: *Get Hep to Love* (1942), *Rhythm of the Islands* (1943) with Acquanetta (wife of an auto dealer in Scottsdale, Arizona), *Kansas City Kitty* (1944), *Calendar Girl* (1947) with Irene Rich [1] (living in Palm Desert, California), *The Gay Ranchero* (1948) with Tito Guizar (living in Mexico City), *Rhythm Inn* (1951) with Lois Collier (married to a Beverly Hills attorney).

Jane became painfully aware of where her career was going when the late Matty Fox, then head of Universal, explained to her that her image and salary dictated that she continue to work in cheapies. Fox brushed aside the comments of critics that she was ready for bigger things with, "We're running a business here."

"I had no great drive to be an important star," she admitted recently, "but I did want to progress and do good work. In the late forties I gave up and began making Roy Rogers pictures which was the beginning of the end." She had been told at one point not to take drama lessons because "then you'll start acting and you won't be any good to us."

Ruth Frazee married producer Norman Krasna and retired early. Jane has a son by the late western star Glenn Tryon who was many years her senior. "We were both looking for security," says Jane.

Jane has remained single since her 1947 divorce from Tryon and lives in Newport Beach, California. She has been a realtor since 1960. Asked if clients often recognize her she replied, "Yes. They say 'Don't you sing in movies? Aren't you that Doris Day?' "

Jane is now a successful real estate broker in Newport Beach, California. *(Jeff Hanna)*

Neil was under contract to Metro-Goldyn-Mayer during the early 1930s.

NEIL HAMILTON

The durable leading man of the screen was born in Lynn, Massachusetts, on September 9, 1899. He spent several years in a stock company and then worked on the assembly line at Ford Motor Company in Detroit before arriving in New York City in 1918.

Almost immediately Hamilton began posing for the top commercial artists of the day. In between modeling jobs he began working as an extra and bit player in some of the silent films then being made in Fort Lee, New Jersey.

The motion picture pioneer D. W. Griffith took a liking to him and he was put under contract to Biograph at a beginning salary of $125 a week. Hamilton is a movie immortal for having appeared in the Griffith classics *The White Rose* (1923), *Isn't Life Wonderful?* (1924), and *America* (1924) with Carol Dempster.[2]

Neil's other silent features include: *The Restless Sex* (1920), *Side Show of Life* (1924) with the late Anna Q. Nilsson,[3] *Beau Geste* (1926), *The Great Gatsby* (1926), and *Why Be Good?* (1929).

The most he was ever paid was $2,500 a week. He worked constantly and had no problem in adjusting to talkies. At M-G-M Irving Thalberg had him grow a mustache and planned to turn him into a heavy. But according to Neil he "told off some of the wrong people." Not only was he dropped from the contract list but he found that no work was open to him except at second- and third-rate studios.

His sound films include: *The Widow From Chicago* (1930), *What Price Hollywood?* (1932), *The World Gone Mad* (1933) with Evelyn Brent [3] and

Mary Brian,[4] *Blind Date* (1934) with Ann Sothern, and *Keeper of the Bees* (1935).

The late thirties and forties were very difficult for Hamilton. The little work he got was at cheapie studios like PRC and Republic. Among his films during that period are *Hollywood Stadium Mystery* (1938) with Evelyn Venable[3] and *Federal Fugitives* (1941) with Victor Varconi (living in Santa Barbara).

In 1943 he was working as a leg man for the agent Paul Kohner for $50 a week and was not even doing a good job at that. He had every intention of committing suicide when a priest talked him into making a novena to the Roman Catholic saint Don Bosco. After nine days of praying he got a part. It was at Universal where years before he had walked off a picture over an imagined slight.

He never came back big but managed to make a living. In the late forties Hamilton starred in the play *State of the Union* in Chicago for two years.

The man who has made 268 motion pictures and played opposite such stars as Joan Crawford, Norma Shearer, Constance Bennett, and Jean Arthur sees none of his contemporaries. The Hamiltons, who have been married since 1922, have no children. They once had a huge home staffed by five servants with the second largest swimming pool in the state of California. Now they share a one-bedroom apartment in a modern but modest building in Escondido. The children in the small Southern California town know Neil as "Commissioner Gordon"—the role he played on the *Batman* TV series. "The adults," says Hamilton, "think I'm Richard Arlen."

Neil beside the painting of himself which appeared on the cover of the *Saturday Evening Post*'s Thanksgiving Day issue in 1918. (*Gawain Bierne-Keyt*)

Lita was fifteen years old when she became Mrs. Charlie Chaplin.

LITA GREY CHAPLIN

The woman who became world famous as the wife of Charlie Chaplin was born Lillita Louise McMurray on April 15, 1908, in Hollywood. Although her parents were divorced when she was eighteen months old, Lita was raised a Roman Catholic.

She first met the superstar of silent pictures in a restaurant where her mother had taken her to celebrate her sixth birthday. She had already seen some of his two-reelers and remembers him seeming "like a god to me." Lita and her mother were bit players in Chaplin's *A Day's Pleasure* (1919) but she had no contact with him during the filming. Two years later she was playing in front of her home when his assistant director spotted her and brought Lita to Chaplin who gave her a part in *The Kid* (1921). Thus began the relationship that resulted in their elopement to Mexico in 1924.

The comedian's new bride was fifteen years old and pregnant. In spite of her age the couple engaged in frequent bitter quarrels in which they were joined by Lita's mother. The part Chaplin promised her in *The Gold Rush* went to Georgia Hale (living in Los Angeles) when she became pregnant for the second time.

They separated in 1926 and were divorced a year later. Lita was left with a sizeable cash settlement and their sons, Charlie, Jr., and Sidney.

After the money was spent Lita toured the country and London in a nightclub act. In 1936 she married a small-time vaudevillian for three months. In 1938 she remarried. When she was divorced ten years later she renounced custody of the seven-year-old boy she and her husband had adopted. In 1949 she made an unsuccessful attempt at a comeback in nightclubs partnered with a young man who was also her lover. Today he is a successful Hollywood producer and still a close friend. In 1956 she began living with another man who was ten years her junior. He left her to marry another woman in 1966 although they are still friends and neighbors.

In 1966 Lita published *My Life with Chaplin: An Intimate Memoir*. It had been turned down by several publishers as being much too intimate. In the book and her interviews to publicize it she told stories of pettiness, greed, and sexual misconduct that many reviewers found repugnant. Readers, however, snapped it up both in hardcover and paperback.

Lita is now at work on a book about her experiences in cheap nightclubs.

When Charlie, Jr., died in 1968 she filed for Social Security claiming he had partially supported her. She, her mother, and her granddaughter share in the income from the trust fund his father had set up for him over forty years ago. It is now worth more than $250,000. In 1970 to keep occupied Lita took the first job of her life and loves it. She is a saleswoman in the better sportswear department of J. W. Robinson's Beverly Hills store. She lives alone in a pretty Hollywood apartment. Her friends, she says, aside from her former husband and ex-lover, are all homosexual men.

Perhaps the most revealing glimpse into the character of Chaplin was given by Lita during a recent interview. Commenting on the fact that both of her boys always preferred Laurel and Hardy to their dad's films she said, "Charlie Chaplin's genius was in comedy. He has no sense of humor, particularly about himself."

Lita is a saleswoman in a Beverly Hills department store. *(James Cury)*

Gargan played charming cads as well as heroes and tough guys.

WILLIAM GARGAN

The actor of stage, screen, radio, and television was born in Brooklyn on July 13, 1905. After he got out of school he worked for a while in his father's profession as a bill collector. After that he was a stockbroker's assistant, a bookmaker, and a salesman.

In 1924 Gargan decided to try acting. His first role was in *Aloma of the South Seas* and he had one line. Before the show closed he had taken over the male lead. After that he did *Laff That Off* (1927) and *War Song* (1928). His big hit on Broadway was in *The Animal Kingdom* (1931). It brought him the Drama Critics Award for the Outstanding Performance of the Year and opened doors wide to him in Hollywood.

In one of the first of his over 100 films he played opposite Joan Crawford in *Rain* (1932). Among the more important pictures he made were: *The Animal Kingdom* (1932), *The Story of Temple Drake* (1933), *Four Frightened People* (1934), *The Milky Way* (1936), *Cheers for Miss Bishop* (1941), *Miss Annie Rooney* (1942) with Shirley Temple, *The Bells of St. Mary's* (1945), and *Miracle in the Rain* (1956). His part as Carole Lombard's lover in *They Knew What They Wanted* (1940) brought him an Academy Award nomination.

In the 1940s he had the title role in three *Ellery Queen* features.

In the early 1950s he brought his *Martin Kane, Private Eye* radio series to television for several seasons.

46

Gargan was a member of what is affectionately known in Hollywood as "the Irish Mafia." He played policemen, priests, reporters, and adventurers with a certain charm and absolutely no nonsense. Some of his lesser efforts were: *Misleading Lady* (1932) with Ben Lyon [4] and the late Lila Lee,[1] *The Crime of Dr. Hallet* (1938) with Josephine Hutchinson (married to actor Staats Cotsworth), *Star Dust* (1940) with Charlotte Greenwood (the widow of a Christian Science teacher lives in Beverly Hills), and *Who Done It?* (1942) with Abbott and Costello.

Bill was coaxed out of retirement in 1960 to play an ex-President who knew he was dying in *The Best Man*. The play was still in out-of-town tryouts when he learned that he had cancer. He had smoked two and a half packs a day.

In his book *Why Me?* (1969) Gargan detailed the mental anguish he suffered after the operation that removed his voice box.

Bill and his wife, who was a dancer in the George White *Scandals*, have been married since 1929. They live in Rancho La Costa in Southern California. One of their two sons is named Leslie Howard Gargan for Bill's costar in *The Male Animal*.

Bill has remained very active. Each year he puts on the La Costa Golf Tournament and is also responsible for a ball in Palm Springs. The proceeds of both go to the Cancer Society. He travels all over the country in attempts to convince other victims that the disease need not be fatal. Bill speaks to audiences with an electric larynx.

Bill makes many appearances for the American Cancer Society.

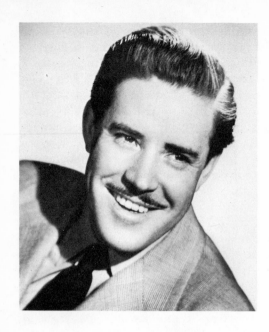

Lon Clark was the only actor ever to play Nick Carter on the Mutual radio series.

NICK CARTER, MASTER DETECTIVE

The private detective hero made his debut over the Mutual Broadcasting Company in 1943. Almost from its debut the program became a listening habit for millions of Americans as they ate their Sunday dinners.

Carter appealed to children and their parents. The latter knew the two-fisted investigator from the Street & Smith dime novels of their youth. Youngsters identified with him because of his keen interest in boys. Nick had founded the Downtown Boys' Club and was always doing what he could to "straighten out" some wayward lad. For a while there was a spin-off character, Chick Carter, Boy Detective, who was featured on his own five-day-a-week, fifteen-minute show. Chick, who was supposed to be Nick's adopted son, was played by both Leon Janney and Billy Lipton.

In all the years *Nick Carter* was on the air Lon Clark played the role for every single broadcast. He had read the books as a boy and knew his character well. One of Carter's strong points was that he was supposed to be able to disguise himself quickly and effectively. Clark was so skilled at changing his own voice he often played several parts other than Nick on the same thirty-minute program. In fact no one ever guessed it was Clark who was heard each week in the show's dramatic opening: a series of hard, frantic knocks on a door. Then—"Yes, what is it?" . . . "It's another case for Nick Carter, Master Detective."

Clark described his character recently as being "a very moral man." Nick did not smoke or drink, and the only woman in his life seemed to be his secretary, Patsy Bowen. Helen Choate played the part until the show went commercial and the sponsor insisted on a more photogenic actress for the fan magazines. Charlotte Manson was chosen. Although there was no romantic interest between Nick and Patsy she was a key figure in the episodes and often led her boss to the criminal.

Clark was a well-established actor before he took over the Nick Carter role. He has remained active since and has also taught courses in poetry, film, and Shakespeare at Adelphi University. He is married and the father of two sons. The Clarks still live in Manhattan where the show used to originate. He is the executive secretary of the Episcopal Actors Guild.

During a recent interview Lon Clark admitted that the series would not be successful today. "Nick epitomized the belief Americans had then about good versus evil. There were no gray areas in those scripts or in Carter's mind."

Nick Carter was one of the last of the dramatic shows to leave the air. About six months before its demise in 1957 an engineer at WOR in New York inadvertently cut it off seconds before it ended. For hours afterward Mutual's switchboards across the country were still jammed by calls from irate listeners demanding to know who the murderer was. The response was so great there were editorials asking "Is radio really dead?" But the show has never returned to the air since 1957.

Radio historian Bill Owen with Lon at WBAI-FM's New York studios. *(Punkin Kohn)*

In 1949 Jack was the host of *Lights Out* on television.

JACK LA RUE

The stage and screen actor known as "The Merchant of Menace" was born Gaspare Biondolillo in New York City on May 3, 1902. As a boy he hung around movie studios until he got a part as a bellboy in a Norma Talmadge starrer. Jack made his debut on Broadway playing a mandolin in *Blood and Sand* (1921) which starred Otis Skinner.

Director Howard Hawks saw La Rue on Broadway in *Midnight* (1930) and brought him to Hollywood to play a heavy in *Scarface*. After three days of shooting it was obvious that Jack had too much authority to be believable as Paul Muni's henchman. He suggested the unknown George Raft [3] to replace him and Raft became a star.

Jack Warner guaranteed the Duke Mantee role in *The Petrified Forest* to him. But its star Leslie Howard had promised it already to Humphrey Bogart who originated the role on Broadway. It was Bogart's springboard to stardom.

The mere presence of Jack La Rue on the screen could set a terrifying mood. He was the mean and sexy tough guy and audiences loved to loathe him. Some of his hundreds of credits are: *The Mouthpiece* (1932), *Good Dame* (1934), *Times Square Lady* (1935), *Captains Courageous* (1937), *Big Town Czar* (1939), *Paper Bullets* (1941), *Murder in the Music Hall* (1946). His swan song was *Robin and the Seven Hoods* (1964).

Now and then he was cast against type as in *A Farewell to Arms* (1932) in which he played a priest. But probably the definitive La Rue was the sadistic abductor of the late Miriam Hopkins in the shocker *The Story of Temple Drake* (1933).

One lady he never threatened was Mae West who had him as her gigolo for three years in *Diamond Lil* (1929) on Broadway and on tour. He was also in her picture *Go West, Young Man* (1936).

He was a great favorite in London and played there in both *Golden Boy* in 1938 and in *Four Hours to Kill* in 1949. He even made an English gangster film, *No Orchids for Miss Blandish* (1951).

Jack has been married and divorced several times. One of his fiancées was Ida Lupino. His only child, Jack, Jr., is also an actor.

In 1969 he sold the Italian restaurant he had operated in North Hollywood. During the nine years he owned it Jack had acquired $187,000 in bad checks and unpaid tabs signed by Hollywood's elite.

The guy who robbed, roughed up, and rubbed out more people than anyone else on the screen abhors violence. He strongly objects to the amount of it which is currently seen on TV. He lives quietly in an apartment he shares with his sister in a high-security building in North Hollywood. Says La Rue, "You've got to be very careful these days. There are some terrible people out there."

Jack shares an apartment with his sister in the San Fernando Valley. *(Scott De Palma)*

In 1939 Virginia was under contract to Metro-Goldwyn-Mayer.

VIRGINIA GREY

The girl who almost made it to stardom was born in Edendale, California, across from the Mack Sennett studios on March 22, 1917. Gloria Swanson often babysat for her mother who edited negatives. Her father, who was a director and Keystone Kop, died when she was five years old.

Paul Kohner saw her at Universal and cast her as Little Eva in *Uncle Tom's Cabin* (1927). After that she worked in bit parts and even as an extra to help out at home. Virginia watched the fun her two sisters had dating and came to resent the career that she had never sought. To make matters worse, during her teens she usually played a floozie. She graduated from high school at M-G-M.

Clark Gable tested with her for a proposed remake of *Saratoga* and she was promised the lead but it was never filmed.

Her Metro contract began at $50 a week. The studio used her frequently but never effectively. Every time a new actor was being screen-tested Virginia was told to play opposite him. There was no one like her and her voice was particularly distinctive but time and again she lost roles that would have put her over. Louis B. Mayer dismissed her pleadings for one part, a second lead, with, "Virginia, you have everything but luck."

Her six-year affair with Clark Gable ended when he eloped with Lady Ashley (living in Pacific Palisades). Virginia told a columnist that for a long time after they broke up she seldom got asked out. "They don't want to be compared to Clark Gable," she explained.

She says *The Rose Tattoo* (1955) was "the most hateful picture I was ever on." But everyone who saw the rushes felt Virginia would have a whole new career as a character woman. She was a shoo-in for the Best Supporting Oscar until at the last minute the studio changed her billing and she wasn't even nominated.

Her friend Ross Hunter has used her often: *The Restless Years* (1958), *Flower Drum Song* (1961), and *Madame X* (1966). But after appearing in over 200 features Virginia still has to travel for a new product development concern to make a living.

Her close friend from the old days is still Lana Turner. Now and then she sees Clark Gable's widow and son who are her neighbors in Encino.

She would like very much to do a TV series but realizes that to new casting people she is just another name. She has found that fans resent that she is not doing something more glamorous when they meet her in places like Iowa. "Listen," she told one, "it doesn't thrill me to pieces either."

Virginia lives alone in Encino, California. *(Michael Knowles)*

In 1930 the RKO publicity department sent out this photo, captioned "Quite a snappy Christmas Carol, eh, wot?"

SUE CAROL

The movie cutie was born Evelyn Lederer on October 30, 1908, in Chicago, Illinois. She attended Kemper Hall in Kenosha, Wisconsin, before her family moved to Los Angeles.

Director Ted Reed spotted her out of 500 high school students on the set of *What a Life* (1926). The late Nick Stuart was then the casting director for Fox Films. He gave Sue a small part in *Slaves of Beauty* (1927). The comedian Douglas MacLean saw her in it and put her under personal contract. They made *Soft Cushions* (1927) together. The picture didn't do well for its star but it was a perfect showcase for Sue Carol.

Her career as an actress was short and profitable. None of her pictures were really important ones but they all exuded the qualities Sue had in abundance—youth, energy, and sex appeal. Among them were: *The Cohens and the Kellys in Paris* (1928), *Girls Gone Wild* (1929) with Johnny Darrow (single and living in Malibu) and David Rollins (single and living in Encinatas, California), *She's My Weakness* (1930) with Arthur Lake,[2] and *Secret Sinners* (1933) with Jack Mulhall.[4] Shortly after making *Straightaway* (1934) she was testing for a feature at Warners when a director told her she was "slow." She walked off that set and has never been in front of a movie camera since. "It wasn't a difficult decision," she said recently. "I never enjoyed acting. But I loved movies—still do."

She became an agent and did fairly well for a while. Then she met a young actor named Alan Ladd. He had been around for a while doing bit parts when she got him a Paramount contract. Until then no one could see him as a leading man because he was exceptionally short. With one picture, *This Gun For Hire* (1942), his career took off. The same year Ladd became Sue's third husband. Sue had been married briefly when very young. Her second husband was Nick Stuart who costarred in many of her films.

Some of her other "discoveries" are Julie London, whom she found running an elevator, and Rory Calhoun, who was riding a horse in Griffith Park. Peter Lawford also got his start with her help.

She has said that she was not nearly as influential in Ladd's career as has been reported. Maybe, but she was certainly instrumental in running up the money he made into a neat fortune. Along with her stock market manipulations, she has a keen eye for choice real estate. Her father had been a developer. The Alan Ladd Hardware Store in the center of Palm Springs is one of her many holdings.

Their Jaguar Productions produced some of his most profitable features: *Hell on Frisco Bay* (1956) and *The Deep Six* (1958). In 1965, a year after Ladd's death, she joined Paramount as a producer.

Sue is a grandmother. She lives in West Los Angeles. Next to being photographed Sue dislikes interviews most.

Sue is now a very attractive business-woman. *(Jon Virzi)*

For seven years straight the *Motion Picture Herald* named Starrett as one of the ten top money-making western stars in the world.

CHARLES STARRETT

The handsome star of over 100 westerns was born in Athol, Massachusetts, on March 28, 1903. At thirteen he ran away to join a theatrical troupe but was brought home and put in a military school. He attended Dartmouth and made quite a name for himself as an athlete. When he appeared as an extra in *The Quarterback* (1926) with Esther Ralston [2] (living in Salem, New York) it only whetted his appetite to become an actor like his hero, Neil Hamilton.

Charles spent two years with the Stuart Walker Stock Company and then tried his luck in New York City where for a while he staged playlets at Wanamaker's Department Store. He appeared in several flops such as *Claire Adams* (1929). Then he got the lead in several low-budget pictures. One was *Damaged Love* (1931) with the late June Collyer. He had a very showy role in *The Mask of Fu Manchu* (1932) and was seen in *So Red the Rose* (1935). But still he was not much of a name. Then Columbia Pictures chose him to replace Col. Tim McCoy (living in Nogales, Arizona).

His career as a cowboy began with *Gallant Defender* (1935) with Len Slye who later became Roy Rogers and ended with *The Kid from Broken Gun* (1952). In between he made between six and eight features a year wearing a white hat and riding his horse Raider. In most of his films he was looked to for protection by Iris Meredith whose dad was usually Ed Le Saint. About the most womenfolk could expect from Starrett was a big polite smile. Lurking somewhere was Dick Curtis who played hulking brutes for all he was worth. There was sometimes a song or two from the *Sons of the Pioneers.*

Starrett was an excellent horseman and a very pleasant man to work with. He was also the best looking good guy in westerns but not in the way that was thought of at the time as being sissified.

In 1940 he played the masked do-gooder *The Durango Kid.* It was so well received it fathered *The Return of the Durango Kid* (1945).

Schedules on Charles Starrett oaters were always tight. Because of this he sometimes found himself with as much as nine months a year in which he was free to pursue his hobbies of hunting and fishing while still drawing a very nice salary. He found no difficulty in adjusting to retirement over twenty years ago. He now spends his winters in his cabin in the High Sierras and the rest of the time in his large home a few steps from the Pacific Ocean in Laguna Beach, California.

He married his childhood sweetheart in 1927. They have twin sons.

At the conclusion of a recent interview he admitted that while his career as a cowpoke provided a very good life he never realized his goal, which was to be a serious actor. He is delighted with the fan mail which still pours in from such places as New Zealand and South Africa. "It's a consolation prize for my old age," said Starrett with a laugh. "My family isn't a bit impressed with my career and my neighbors think I'm one of them—a retired businessman."

Charles is completely retired and living in Laguna Beach, California. *(Jimmy Eason)*

The late Walter Winchell used to refer to Virginia as "the most beautiful blonde in the world."

VIRGINIA FIELD

The movie and stage actress whom Walter Winchell used to call "the most beautiful blonde in the world" was born Margaret St. John Field in London on November 4, 1917. Her mother was a descendant of General Robert E. Lee and her father was a prominent English judge.

Most of Virginia's schooling took place on the Continent. Max Reinhardt, whom she met in Vienna, presented her in his production of *All's Well that Ends Well*.

Her first movie was the English-made *The Lady Is Willing* (1934). Gilbert Miller was about to present her to Broadway audiences in a featured role in *Victoria Regina* when she was offered a Hollywood contract.

During the years she spent at Twentieth Century-Fox Virginia was always overshadowed by the flashier blondes under contract to that studio. The best she was usually able to manage were roles as "the other woman." She could act, she had poise and style, and could deliver a key line with great precision, but Virginia Field never became a star. Some feel it was her candid opinions that held her back.

David O. Selznick picked her for his prestigious *Little Lord Fauntleroy* (1936) and then made a pass at her. Virginia's reaction was to hit him over the head with a decanter.

She told interviewers Al Raker and Doug McClelland that although she made three films with Loretta Young she was "the only actress I really disliked. She was sickeningly sweet, a pure phony. Her two faces sent me home angry and crying several times."

Virginia remembers Betty Hutton from their work together on Broadway in *Panama Hattie* (1940) and in the picture *Dream Girl* (1948): "Very moody, with constant up and down periods."

Miss Field's busy life off screen may have been another reason she didn't make it any bigger than she did. She was married to the late Paul Douglas from 1942 to 1946. They have a daughter who is working as an actress in England. The year after their divorce she married composer Howard Grode for all of three months. Since 1951 Virginia has been the wife of former actor Willard Parker.

She was in over 40 pictures including: *Lloyds of London* (1936), *Captain Fury* (1939), *Waterloo Bridge* (1940), *Crystal Ball* (1943), *The Perfect Marriage* (1946), *A Connecticut Yankee in King Arthur's Court* (1949), and *Appointment with a Shadow* (1958). She was also one of *The Doughgirls* on Broadway in 1942.

Until 1974 her husband was a prosperous real estate dealer in Indian Wells, near Palm Springs, and Virginia owned a boutique near his office. His serious stroke changed everything. "Overnight," she said recently, "my life was turned upside down. But then I've coped with difficulties before and I intend to manage with this one."

Virginia now plans to resume her career which ended with the feature *The Earth Dies Screaming* (1964).

Virginia plans to resume her career soon. *(Alice Barr)*

John Bubbles (left) and his partner Buck were a show business team for over forty years. *(Michael Knowles Collection)*

JOHN BUBBLES

The surviving member of the once popular dance and comedy team Buck and Bubbles was born in Louisville, Kentucky, on February 19, 1902. His real name is John William Sublett. When he was seven years old Bubbles began singing on amateur nights at the all-black theatre in his home town. Later he spent a year touring with a carnival.

John and Buck were still in their teens when they met while setting pins in a bowling alley.

When they first appeared at the Mary Anderson Theatre in Louisville there had never been a black even on the first floor much less on stage. While they were the first to break the race barrier there, they had to wear black face so the audience would think they were white.

For the first few years they made so little money that their suits and shoes fit poorly and became part of their comedy routines. After they made a success their clothes were impeccable and were a hallmark of their act. People still laughed but it was at their patter. No one ever dressed better than Buck and Bubbles.

It was during a benefit they played at a New York City burlesque house that they really caught on. That was 1920 and within two months they were booked into the Palace Theatre.

By the time Buck and Bubbles signed to appear in the *Ziegfeld Follies of 1931* they had been on Broadway in *Frolics of 1922*, had made movie shorts, had given a command performance for the King of England, and been the personal guests of the Prince of Wales. After they took a salary cut from the $1,750 a week they made in vaudeville to $800 they were given the worst spot in the show and a dressing room in the basement. Audiences and critics however gave them the sweetest possible revenge. They proved to be the hit of the show.

The team separated for a while when Bubbles played Sportin' Life in the original production of *Porgy and Bess* (1935).

On January 31, 1955, Buck died. His real name was Ford Lee Washington. Bubbles worked sporadically afterward on TV shows. In 1967 after he had closed with Judy Garland at the Palace Theatre he suffered a stroke.

Today John is single. He lives in a small modern house in Los Angeles and has a housekeeper to look after him. "Had I saved a lot of money," he says, "I wouldn't know what I know now."

The reputation of Buck and Bubbles is still of legendary proportions and the dance steps they created are still being used. One of their contemporaries recently said of the duo: "They were an act no one wanted to follow and they made some of the best of us feel a bit tacky. Those were two very classy guys."

John Bubbles is completely retired and living in Los Angeles. *(Michael Knowles)*

Billy and Bobby made the cover of *Time* magazine on May 8, 1937.

THE MAUCH TWINS

The identical twins of movies and radio were born on July 6, 1942, in Peoria, Illinois. Their mother was ambitious for them from the beginning and by the time they were three years old the Mauchs were known locally for their singing and dancing act which they did at benefits and parties.

In 1932 Mrs. Mauch (their name rhymes with "talk"), whose husband was an agent for the Toledo, Peoria & Western Railroad, took the boys to New York City where they got work immediately as models. It was through their parts on radio shows like *Let's Pretend* and *March of Time* that they came to the attention of Warner Brothers. The studio signed Billy for *Anthony Adverse* (1936) mainly because of the twins' resemblance to the film's star, Fredric March. Bobby was to be his stand-in but when the picture was finished the twins informed director Mervyn Le Roy that they had switched whenever the mood struck them. The only perceptible difference between them is that Billy, who is ten minutes older, is left-handed while Bobby uses his right.

The studio offered Billy a contract but Mrs. Mauch insisted that they both be signed. When Warners demurred she threatened to sign Bobby to a rival studio. They were both placed under contract at $350 a week each with an added $150 a week for Mrs. Mauch as their guardian.

Their big year was 1937. *Time* magazine carried their photos on its cover and did a feature article on their movie *The Prince and the Pauper*. Its director William Keighley (married to Genevieve Tobin [4] and living in Manhattan) thought he was using Billy for all the palace scenes and Bobby as the pauper but again the pair amused themselves by changing roles.

Their studio put them in a series based on the Booth Tarkington books: *Penrod and Sam* (1937), *Penrod's Double Trouble* (1938), and *Penrod and His Twin Brother* (1938). Their last before World War II was *Double Trouble* (1941).

There is a ruling in the Armed Forces that twins cannot be separated unless they request it. Billy and Bobby were seen for a time in the *Winged Victory* service show and then served in the Air Force in the Philippines.

Bob realized that their novelty would get them little work as adults and went into film editing upon their discharge. Bill tried it alone for five years but made little impact in such features as *That Hagen Girl* (1947) and *Roseanna McCoy* (1949) with Joan Evans (owner of a private school in Van Nuys, California).

The brothers have remained very close and are still recognized by fans when they go out together. Bob, a divorcé, edited TV commercials and many of the *Dragnet* series. He is semi-retired and lives now in Big Bear, California. Bill married a girl he had known since he was five years old. They have one son and live in Woodland Hills, California. He is a sound editor at his home lot, Warner Brothers.

Both twins admit that they still have a twinge when they think about the abrupt end to their career. Asked if anything would induce them to act again Bill replied recently, "Yes, we would love to play the Collier brothers."

Billy is a sound editor with his old studio, Warner Brothers. *(Jon Virzi)*

Bob is now semi-retired. *(Jon Virzi)*

By the late 1930s Jane had become one of the most popular radio singers in America.

JANE FROMAN

The popular singer was born November 10, 1907, in St. Louis, Missouri. After studying journalism at the University of Missouri she attended Cincinnati's Conservatory of Music. Her mother was an accomplished pianist and a teacher of music who encouraged her daughter to pursue a career.

Her first job was singing over WLW in Cincinnati at a salary of $85 a week. Jane was Paul Whiteman's vocalist briefly before being brought to Hollywood by Warner Brothers. After flunking three screen tests the studio sent her to an elocution teacher to correct her stuttering. She made only two pictures, *Stars Over Broadway* (1935) and *Radio City Revels* (1938), and didn't click in either. That however was no disappointment to her. She had refused to abide by the rules of the Hollywood caste system and disliked the movie capital's phoniness and values.

By the late thirties it was clear that Jane Froman was a big hit with radio audiences. Her name topped the popularity polls several times. She was seen on Broadway in *Ziegfeld Follies of 1934* and *Keep Off the Grass* (1940).

Jane had a rare combination of qualities as a performer. For all her polished style and chic clothes the years she spent in America's heartland were also very apparent in her act which had elegance but was never pretentious.

At 6:36 P.M. on February 22, 1943, a Pan Am plane carrying Jane's U.S.O. troupe crashed into icy waters off the coast of Lisbon, Portugal. By V-E Day she was back in front of the G.I.s in a motorized wheelchair for a 3½-month, 30,000-mile tour. She wore a flowing gown to conceal a 30-pound cast on her leg. In the accident one ankle had been crushed and the other leg had a compound fracture.

A film dramatization of her ordeal, *With a Song in My Heart,* was one of the hits of 1952. Susan Hayward mouthed the songs which Jane dubbed in a rich contralto. As in the movie Jane did divorce her singer-husband Don Ross to marry the co-pilot who saved her life after the crash. But by 1956 they were divorced.

The popularity Jane Froman enjoyed for sixteen years after the crash was enormous. In nightclubs she commanded $8,000 a week and the Roxy Theatre paid her $10,000. During the 1950s she hosted a TV show for General Electric for three seasons. Even people not usually interested in performers were impressed by her courage and charmed by her warmth.

In 1959 she called it quits and retired to the college town of Columbia, Missouri. In 1962 she married a member of the administration of her alma mater. She had known him in college but in those days he never got up the nerve to ask her to dance. In spite of the heavy brace she wears Jane is an ardent golfer. Her other hobbies are bridge and cooking. She has remained close with her two friends, Ireene Wicker, radio's *Singing Lady,*[2] and Jean Muir (head of the drama department of Stevens College).

Jane has undergone 38 separate major operations and had numerous bone grafts for which she has paid over $400,000 of her own money. She lost her suit against Pan Am and it took an act of Congress in 1957 to recoup any medical expenses from the U.S. government. The amount she received was $20,000.

"The hardest part of it all," said Jane recently, "was to keep from becoming bitter. Thank God I licked that long ago." Ms. Froman has been in constant pain since the day of the crash.

Jane today in her home in Columbia, Missouri. *(Michael Knowles)*

Iturbi played himself in the 1942 movie
musical *Thousands Cheer.*

JOSE ITURBI

The pianist-conductor movie personality was born on November 28, 1895,
just hours after his mother had sung *Carmen* before a large audience in
Valencia, Spain. His father was a piano technician. Although neither
parent encouraged Jose to study music he began to play the piano at
three years old and by 1900 was taking lessons. At age seven he performed
in cinemas and recitals. He was in his early teens when he left home to
study in Paris.

The late Wanda Landowska was one of his early champions and by
1919 he became head of the Geneva Conservatory's piano school, a position
once held by Franz Liszt.

In October of 1929 Iturbi debuted in the United States with the Philadelphia Orchestra under Leopold Stokowski. He has lived in America
ever since and became a citizen in 1943.

In 1933 he began conducting and for a number of years led the Rochester
Philharmonic Orchestra.

Although he never achieved the artistry of a Horowitz or Rubinstein
he is a much finer musician than many in the music world will admit.
Jose's penchant for public squabbles, always fully reported in the press,
and his flamboyant showmanship have kept him the subject of criticism
among his colleagues. Once a program which he was conducting was
cut off the air because he objected to the songs Jan Peerce and Lucy
Monroe (living on Manhattan's Sutton Place) planned to sing. At a 1941
concert he played Liszt while at the same time conducting the orchestra,
keeping the beat at times with his head. The same year he refused to appear
on the same stage with Benny Goodman explaining that while he ap-
preciated all music he disapproved of mixing swing with Stravinsky.

In 1943 a Los Angeles court awarded him custody of his grandchildren when he charged his daughter was unfit to raise them. Iturbi had reconciled with his only child, Maria, when she committed suicide three years later.

His greatest sin may have been his appearance in six M-G-M musicals. What compounded the criticism within his profession was not so much that he played boogie-woogie along with the classics but that the movie camera captured the charm that had long made him a favorite with concert audiences. People who neither knew nor cared about serious music knew who Jose Iturbi was from his pictures such as: *Two Girls and a Sailor* (1944), *Holiday in Mexico* (1946), and *That Midnight Kiss* (1949). It was Iturbi who dubbed Cornel Wilde's playing in *A Song to Remember* (1945).

He adamantly refuses to discuss any aspect of his movie career.

His recordings still sell well and his rendition of Chopin's *Polonaise* has gone beyond the two million mark.

Although he still performs, his heart condition has placed serious limitations on his career. He is a widower and lives in a 12-room Beverly Hills mansion once occupied by Mrs. McLean, owner of the Hope diamond.

The artist who once outraged much of his public and profession by stating that women musicians were physically and temperamentally handicapped told an interviewer recently that he is now able to admit that his late sister Ampar, who was overshadowed by her colorful brother throughout her career, was always the better pianist.

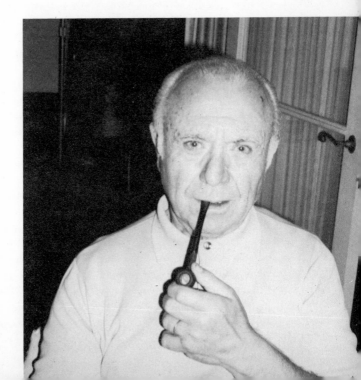

Jose Iturbi at home in his mansion in Beverly Hills. *(Don Atkins)*

Jane Bryan in 1939, one year before she quit pictures.

JANE BRYAN

The almost star was born Jane O'Brian in Los Angeles on June 11, 1918. Her original goal was the stage and she began studying with Jean Muir's Hollywood Theatre Workshop. She wasn't there long before Warner Brothers put her under contract.

From the beginning the studio had high hopes for her and almost everything she did proved their expectations were going to be fulfilled. She held her own among a cast of top pros in *The Marked Woman* (1937) and *A Slight Case of Murder* (1938). Those who felt she had been signed as a threat to Bette Davis got quite a surprise when the queen of the lot adopted her as a protégé. In fact when Bette was once asked if she felt Jane could carry a heavy dramatic role the star replied with a laugh, "The last time I played with her I had to hide her face in a pillow to keep her from stealing my scenes."

Many felt that while Bette Davis and the late Miriam Hopkins were pulling every trick they knew on each other while making *The Old Maid* (1939), Jane quietly walked away with the picture. Some critics said she stole *We Are Not Alone* (1939) from Paul Muni who at that time was considered one of the country's greatest actors.

Jane was unaffected when few were and underplayed when almost no one did. Noel Coward once stopped her on the street to tell her he thought she was the best young actress in America.

Some of her pictures were: *The Case of the Black Cat* (1936), *Confession* (1937), *The Sisters* (1938), *Brother Rat* (1938), *Each Dawn I Die* (1939), *Invisible Stripes* (1940), and *Brother Rat and a Baby* (1940).

A *Life* magazine article said she was "critical of herself and shuns publicity." Like almost everyone it predicted major stardom. But Jane's father was a lawyer and she never pursued her career out of financial need. When she walked away from it, as she did when she married in 1939, she proved she had no emotional need for acting. She has never returned nor does she now grant interviews.

Her life since her retirement has been as a mother to her two boys and one girl and a wife to Justin Dart, the chairman of the board of a huge conglomerate which controls, among many other corporations, all the Rexall products and stores. He is also a noted philanthropist. Jane is very active in charity work and travels constantly with Dart. They are Roman Catholics.

A recent column by Hollywood reporter Hank Grant summed up filmdom's awe of Jane thusly: "She is the only actress within my memory who gave up her successful career for marriage and motherhood and is still happily married without a single regretful look at her past."

Jane Bryan fooled all of Hollywood by having the courage when she arrived at the very brink of major stardom to say "No thank you" and mean it.

Mrs. Justin Dart, Irene Dunne Griffin. (*Los Angeles* Times)

Lili took a few liberties when she played Pocahontas in her nightclub act. *(Culver Pictures)*

LILI ST. CYR

The star striptease was born Marie Van Schaak in Minneapolis, Minnesota, on June 3, 1917. Her body, which was one of the most memorable ever revealed before the public, was developed with early ballet lessons. She was brought up in Pasadena, California.

A photographer discovered the fifteen-year-old Lili waiting on tables and asked her to model. From that she got a job in the chorus line of Nils T. Granlund's Florentine Gardens. She was there for three years before an agent realized her potential and promoted her into the biggest star in burlesque.

Lili was one of the very few peelers who got out of burlesque without putting their clothes on. It was done with very smart management and a fortune in Christian Dior gowns and jewels. Her act was just too classy to stay in the bump-and-grind houses. When she did play them the audiences did not stomp and whistle as they did at other burlesque queens. They were in awe of Lili who was more than merely sexy. She was highly erotic.

She made as much as $7,500 a week in the country's top supper clubs. In the act she was a little girl who gets up in the morning, slips out of her nightie and into a bathtub. Only her bathtub had a glass front and a lot of bubbles—but not too many. She often did sketches playing Cleopatra, Carmen, Eve, or Aphrodite. She even made movies such as *The Miami Story* (1954) and *Son of Sinbad* (1955).

As early as 1954 she announced her retirement but she continued for over a decade. By 1964 when her life story was being syndicated in newspapers she had already earned over $3 million.

In 1951 when she was arrested for lewdness on stage the late attorney Jerry Geisler got her off by making the whole matter a joke in the eyes of the jury. It cost her $2,000 and reaped a million dollars' worth of publicity.

Lili shed her husbands almost as quickly as her clothes. She has been married to a motorcycle racer, a waiter, a dancer-singer, a movie sound man, an actor, and a restauranteur. She never accepted alimony after any of her seven divorces and has stayed friendly with all her ex-husbands.

As early as 1958 she had attempted suicide. When she finally quit in the mid-sixties it was because of a severe nervous breakdown.

She sees almost no one from show business and her home in the Hollywood Hills is secluded behind tall trees.

The lady who was called "an ecdysiast" in her heyday now describes herself as a housewife. She takes in stray cats and at times has had as many as ten of them. She is a gourmet cook and reads about a book a day, curled up in front of one of her five fireplaces.

After her famous bath Lili would get dressed in front of her audiences. No performer ever appealed more to fetishists than she did. Today her shop in West Hollywood and its mail order line, The Undie-World of Lili St. Cyr, still does a brisk business in highly abbreviated lingerie.

Lili lives quietly in the Hollywood Hills with a collection of stray cats and her eighth husband. *(Ron Vogel)*

Bill was under contract to M-G-M when he enlisted in the Marine Corps in 1943.

WILLIAM LUNDIGAN

The handsome movie actor was born on June 12, 1914, in Syracuse, New York. When he was ten years old he began to work around radio station WFBL. By the time he was in high school he was announcing and producing three kiddie shows a week. His emcee was an even younger Gordon MacRae. Bill continued radio work while he attended the University of Syracuse.

A press agent suggested him to Universal Pictures. The studio liked his looks but were particularly impressed by the resonant voice and diction. He was brought to Hollywood in 1937. He was working on his first feature, *Armored Car* (1937), when he offered to quit rather than accept the new name that had been chosen for him. He was to be called Larry Parks.

When Warner Brothers borrowed him to play Olivia de Havilland's brother in *Dodge City* (1939) he stayed on for two years. The only showy part Universal had given him was in *Three Smart Girls Grow Up* (1939). He did little better at Warners except for *The Old Maid* (1939), *The Sea Hawk* (1940), and *The Fighting 69th* (1940).

When he went to M-G-M they talked of his taking over the *Dr. Kildare* series but instead he was given run-of-the-mill programmers, except for two Andy Hardy features. When he finished making *A Salute to the Marines* (1943) he became one and served on Okinawa.

In 1945 Metro welcomed Lundigan back from the service by dropping his option. He free-lanced in *Dishonored Lady* and *The Fabulous Dorseys* in 1947 and then went under contract to Twentieth Century-Fox. In his five years there the two most important things he did were to be in the controversial *Pinky* (1949) and to put his hands in the cement in front of Grauman's Chinese Theatre.

Bill survived over 100 B pictures and some that only seemed like B's such as *Down Among the Sheltering Palms* (1953). "My mistake," he admits, "was in being so damned cooperative. Not only did I accept the bad pictures but I accepted lousy parts in those bad pictures."

It was however the likeable image built in bland roles that put him over on TV in the 1950s. He became "Mr. Chrysler" as host of their prestigious playhouse *Climax* and on their commercials. He thoroughly enjoyed it and made a lot of money but when it was over he was hopelessly identified with one product.

Bill's pictures during the sixties were two cheapies and the $10 million flop *The Way West* (1967).

The Lundigans and their adopted daughter live in an apartment in Westwood, California. Although ill health during recent years has minimized his socializing he is very active in fund-raising for the Cystic Fibrosis Foundation.

The man he describes himself as being sounds not unlike the part he so often played: "I'm a square, conservative Irishman and I make no apologies for it."

Anastacia and Bill Lundigan in West Los Angeles. *(Jeff Hanna)*

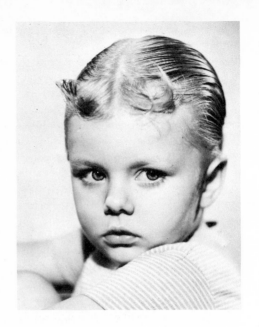

Larry played Baby Dumpling, or Alexander Bumstead, in 28 *Blondie* movies.

LARRY SIMMS
"BABY DUMPLING"

The boy who became world famous playing the son of Arthur Lake and Penny Singleton in the *Blondie* movies was born in Santa Monica on October 1, 1934. His mother sang under the name Margaret Lawrence with Jimmy Greer's band at the Coconut Grove.

When Larry was three years old he modeled for the cover of the *Saturday Evening Post*. Someone at Columbia Pictures spotted his picture and suggested him for the part of Baby Dumpling, a character in the Bumstead family. The studio was about to make films of the highly popular *Blondie* comic strip created by the late Chic Young. The day they finished shooting the first of the features, *Blondie* (1938), the cast presented Larry with a big cake and a tricycle. It was his fourth birthday.

The pictures were always considered B's but were very popular due chiefly to the casting. Later Marjorie Ann Mutchie was added to the cast playing Baby Dumpling's little sister Cookie. It was about this time that Larry became Alexander. In a recent interview he explained what that change meant: "There was never anything about picture making that turned me on or off. It was just something I did. But when Baby Dumpling changed to Alexander, that was the high point of the whole experience for me. It meant that I got to wear long pants."

Larry made a few pictures besides the 28 *Blondie* films: *Mr. Smith Goes to Washington* (1939), *The Gay Sisters* (1942), *Golden Earrings* (1947), and *Madame Bovary* (1949).

He had no particular interest in movies and saw only a few of his own. Larry spent all of his spare time with the studio technicians. He wasn't a bit disappointed when the series came to an end with *Beware of Blondie* in 1950. He did not consider himself a natural actor and no effort was made to get him other roles.

Larry made no close friends among the actors he worked with but when he was married at age eighteen Penny Singleton [2] came to the wedding. He hasn't seen her or Arthur Lake [2] in many years. "Everyone at the studio was nice to me," says Larry. "But they were all adults. When there were parties on the lot I got to stir the cocktails and eat an occasional maraschino cherry."

When he was six years old his father and mother were divorced.

His salary, which reached as high as $750 a week, went to educate and support him and his younger brother. Says Larry, "Michael never complained but I know there must have been times when he felt left out. I was always the one who got the attention. It used to worry me."

After getting out of the Navy he studied aeronautical engineering at California Polytechnic. When he was only twenty-two Larry was in charge of one of the three overseas tracking stations for Explorer I. He has been an engineer at the Jet Propulsion Lab in Pasadena since 1956.

Baby Dumpling has been divorced twice. The oldest of his three children is married. Larry lives alone on a cruising sailboat in the Los Angeles harbor.

Larry with Richard Lamparski's St. Bernard, whose name is Baby Dumpling. *(Travis W. Armstrong)*

It was the late Quentin Reynolds who gave Anita the title "The Face." *(NBC Photo)*

ANITA COLBY

The model who was nationally famous as "The Face" was born Anita Katherine Counihan in Washington, D.C., on August 5, 1914. Her father was the Pulitzer Prize winning Bud Counihan whose cartoons appeared in Hearst newspapers. Anita's home atmosphere and schooling were strictly Roman Catholic.

It was at a school prom that she chose her profession. A classmate who had done some modeling stole the show. Shortly afterward Anita became a John Robert Powers model at $5.00 an hour. Eventually she was the first model to be paid twenty times that sum.

Anita popularized the black pillbox hat, launched a new ship with a $1,000 bottle of perfume, and was within one month on the cover of 38 different magazines. In 1945 "The Face" was on the cover of *Time*. In 1947 her total income was $100,000.

Anita appeared in a few movies: *Mary of Scotland* (1936) and *Brute Force* (1947). In *Cover Girl* (1944) she not only played herself but designed some of the clothes and worked on the script. At different times she was a consultant to both David O. Selznick and Paramount Pictures. Both took her high-priced advice very seriously. She was responsible for the images of a number of top female stars.

Millions of women followed her advice which she dispensed with charm and humor in the syndicated column *Anita Says* and a beauty book. When she became president and editor of the Women's News Service it was getting into five newspapers. When she left it in 1960 it was being picked up by 100.

During the 1950s Anita was seen frequently on TV programs as an interviewer and panelist. For six months in 1961 she had a daily spot on *Today*.

She dated luminaries such as Jimmy Stewart and Clark Gable but remained single until New Year's Eve 1970. Anita and her husband, who is a vice-president of the J. P. Stevens Company, have an estate in the farmlands of New Jersey. When they are in Manhattan Mr. & Mrs. Palen Flagler stay at the exclusive River Club. She is an enthusiastic art collector and spends a great deal of time painting as a hobby.

Although her friendships with celebrities like Ernest Hemingway, Quentin Reynolds, and Pablo Picasso were well known, she showed a skill, rare in such a public personality, in keeping her personal life private. Anita is credited with bringing her friend Winston Churchill together with his favorite movie star, Greta Garbo.

A fashion executive and contemporary of Anita's said of her recently, "She didn't seem to need the usual scandals or bitchiness to make her what she became. I can't think of anyone in her profession who was so envied—and in the nicest of ways. She has the *real* chic. It's from within her."

Anita is still very much a part of the New York social scene. (*Al Levine*)

In 1934 Gail was under contract to Paramount Pictures.

GAIL PATRICK

The attractive movie actress was born Margaret Fitzpatrick on June 20, in Birmingham, Alabama. Her intent while studying law at the University of Alabama's night school was to become the governor of her state. Before passing the bar examination, however, she won a local newspaper contest and was sent to Hollywood for a week. She had entered as a lark and when she found that she had been chosen Birmingham's "Panther Girl," she had to borrow clothes for the trip.

Although she was not the contest's national winner, Paramount Pictures offered to sign her at $50 a week. "My dad never made more than $175 a month in his life," she said recently. "I got them up to $75 a week and grabbed that contract."

While Gail never became a star she was usually more than competent and at times a sheer delight in the many pictures she made, beginning with *The Mysterious Rider* (1933). Her others include: *Doubting Thomas* (1935) with Sterling Holloway,[3] *Murder With Pictures* (1936) with Joyce Compton,[3] *John Meade's Woman* (1937) with Francine Larrimore (living in Manhattan), *My Favorite Wife* (1940), *Gallant Sons* (1940) with Tommy Kelly (living in Venice, California) and Ian Hunter (living in an actor's home in Middlesex, England), *Hitler's Children* (1943) with Tala Birell (rumored to have died behind the Iron Curtain), *Up in Mabel's Room* (1944), and *Claudia and David* (1946).

Gail retired from acting in 1947 when she married Cornwall Jackson, Erle Stanley Gardner's literary agent, and for a while had a children's clothing shop in Beverly Hills. Then in 1956 the Jacksons began the *Perry Mason* series on CBS Television. It ran on the network until 1965 and is still one of the most viewed programs in syndication around the world. By 1970 it had grossed $20 million. Gail had been executive producer of the original series and although she and Jackson had a bitter divorce in 1969, she was retained as a consultant when the series was revived unsuccessfully in 1973. She is now developing another Gardner property, *Lamb Cool*, for TV on her own.

Gail Patrick is a diabetic. Both her son and daughter are adopted. She lives on a large estate in Hollywood that she bought from the estate of Mark Hellinger (his widow, Ziegfeld beauty Gladys Glad, lives in Manhattan).

The only time she has ever seen herself on the screen was recently when a friend presented her with a print of *My Man Godfrey* (1936). Asked about her reaction she replied: "I always felt self-conscious as an actress because I'm tall. I see that it came over as haughtiness. I just don't have an actress' soul. I think mine has a dollar sign on it."

Gail is now a highly successful businesswoman. *(Peter Cury)*

King Vidor directed Jean in *The Texas Rangers* in 1936.

JEAN PARKER

The movie star of the 1930s and 1940s was born Luis Stephanie Zelinska in Butte, Montana, on August 11, 1915. After her father left when she was still a very little girl, Jean's mother brought her to Pasadena, California, where she grew up.

She was discovered for the movies when she was still in junior high school. Jean had won a poster contest and Ida Koverman, secretary to Louis B. Mayer, saw her photo in the newspaper and brought it to her boss's attention. She was screen-tested, put under contract, and finished her education at M-G-M's Little Red School House.

The first of her 72 feature films was *Divorce in the Family* (1932). Then after three winners, *Little Women* (1933), *Sequoia* (1934), and *The Ghost Goes West* (1936), she left Metro. She made A pictures afterward but was usually in the shadow of her leading men such as Edward G. Robinson, Robert Taylor, Charles Boyer, or George Raft.[3] And there were plenty of cheapies: *A Wicked Woman* (1934) with Bill Henry (a landscape architect in the San Fernando Valley), *Romance of the Limberlost* (1938), *The Gunfighter* (1950), and *The Parson and the Outlaw* (1957). Monogram Pictures attempted to tailor a detective series around her as Kitty O'Day, but only two were made.

Her first husband was a newspaperman, her second was radio commentator Douglas Daw, and the third was a studio executive. Her last marriage was to Robert Lowery, who at the time was considered "the king of the B pictures." They were divorced in 1958 after eight years but remained friends until he died on Christmas Day, 1971. Their son is now in law school.

Jean Parker's career is a curious one. She was very popular, especially among teenagers, but she never fulfilled the potential many saw in her. She survived as a screen actress until *Apache Uprising* (1966) in which she was billed eleventh.

Her best work was done on the stage in the late forties and early fifties. Her notices for *Dream Girl, Burlesque,* and *Born Yesterday* were excellent. Many who saw her in the last feel she was even better than Judy Holliday. But her one big shot at Broadway, *Loco* (1946), was a flop.

Jean lives in an apartment in Eagle Rock only ten miles from Hollywood but seldom sees any of her contemporaries. She recently did a radio commercial for a Los Angeles savings and loan company and occasionally works as an acting coach. She says she is working on a book on acting technique.

Jean on a recent evening on the town. *(Frank Edwards)*

Russell played Lucky in nearly forty of the Hopalong Cassidy westerns.

RUSSELL HAYDEN

The western star who rose to fame as Hopalong Cassidy's sidekick was born Hayden Michael Lucid on June 10, 1912, on a 640-acre ranch in Chico, California. Russell's family moved all over the West while he was growing up. He left home as a teenager and took night classes while he worked at a variety of jobs.

Finally he was hired in the lab at Paramount Pictures. From there he became business manager for Harry "Pop" Sherman, producer of the Hopalong Cassidy features. When James Ellison, who played the part of the late William Boyd's [2] young friend in the series, left, Russell made his debut in *The Hills of Old Wyoming* (1937). With that film and the nearly forty Hopalong pictures that followed Hayden became identified forever in the minds of western fans as Lucky Jenkins. While the dialogue at times left a bit to be desired the character was well developed and Russell played it with great charm. His horse in the pictures was named Banjo. Although Hoppy was always courtly with the ladies he never had much time for them. Lucky however had an eye for them and a way with them.

Paramount gave him his own series of Zane Grey westerns: *Mysterious Rider* (1938), *Heritage of the Desert* (1939), and *Knights of the Range* (1940). But the money Columbia Pictures offered him was too tempting and he began starring for the Gower Street lot in *The Lone Prairie* (1942). Some of his later efforts were: *Gambler's Choice* (1944), *Apache Chief* (1949), and *Texans Never Cry* (1951). At Columbia he always had someone like Adele Mara or Ann Savage to win or wait for him. In *Rolling Home* (1948) it was Jean Parker.

He quit acting in the early fifties to produce low-budget westerns. Later he branched out into directing and TV. His *26 Men* was on ABC-TV from 1957 to 1959 and the *Judge Roy Bean* series was also his.

Russell and his wife, former starlet Lillian Porter, whom he married in 1946, live in North Hollywood when they are not at their 200-acre ranch near Palm Springs. Although almost blind, Hayden plans to open it to the public soon as "Old Pioneer Town." Along with Lucky to draw the crowds are over $250,000 worth of western antiques that have been used in making oaters including authentic stagecoaches, costumes of famous cowboy stars, and personal appearances by his old friends like "Fuzzy" Knight (living in Hollywood).

His only child by his first wife, Jan Clayton, who played Tommy Rettig's [4] mother on TV's *Lassie* series, was killed some years ago when the new Cadillac her parents had bought her collided with another car.

Russell divides his time now between North Hollywood and Palm Springs. *(Robert G. Youngson)*

Another of Adele's titles was *The Girl With the Million Dollar Legs*.

ADELE JERGENS

The glamour girl of stage and screen was born Adele Louisa Jergens on November 26, 1917, in the Ridgewood section of Brooklyn. At seven years old she began taking dancing lessons and by the time she reached fourteen Adele won a scholarship to the Albertina Rasch Dance School. After graduating from Rockville Center High School she spent a week in the chorus of the Brooklyn Fox Theatre before becoming a Powers model. Her days were spent modeling the latest creations of New York and Paris while at night she appeared on Broadway in such shows as *Jubilee (1935)*, *DuBarry Was a Lady* (1939), *Louisiana Purchase* (1940), and *Banjo Eyes* (1941).

By 1939 Adele was one of the top models and showgirls in New York. Nils T. Granlund was one of her biggest boosters. She toured Paris, London, and Rio de Janeiro and during the 1939 World's Fair was dubbed Miss World's Fairest.

Adele spent a year under contract to Twentieth Century-Fox doing bit parts. She returned to Broadway to understudy the late Gypsy Rose Lee in *Star and Garter* (1942). One night when she went on for the star a talent scout for Columbia Pictures saw her. The studio put her under contract and she started out in a small role in *Together Again* (1944). Her first real part came as the lead in the serial *Black Arrow* (1944).

Many felt Adele was signed by Columbia to keep their number-one star, Rita Hayworth, in line. They made *Tonight and Every Night* (1945) and *Down to Earth* (1947) together but were never friends.

Adele made both A and B features but usually had ·to be content to play second leads. Her movies include: *She Wouldn't Say Yes* (1945), *The Corpse Came C.O.D.* (1947), *The Fuller Brush Man* (1948), *Ladies of the Chorus* (1949), *The Sound of Fury* (1950), and *Aaron Slick from Punkin' Crick* (1951). Her last was *Lonesome Trail* (1958).

Where Adele Jergens was not slighted was publicity. Press agents dubbed her "The Eyeful" and "The Champagne Blonde." She was one of the leading pinups of the 1940s.

In 1949 she made *Treasure of Monte Cristo* opposite Glenn Langan. They were married the same year. They were also together in *The Big Chase* (1954) but by then their only child had been born and she wanted to be with him as much as possible. One of her last exposures was as a regular on Mike Stokey's (living in Los Angeles) *Pantomine Quiz,* the TV show of the fifties.

Her husband travels a great deal in his work for a San Francisco based corporation and her son no longer lives at home. Adele admits she wouldn't mind working again but is well aware that she is too old to play glamour girls anymore. The Langans live in a house in the San Fernando Valley which was once a telegraph station for the Pony Express Company.

Tracy, Adele, and Glenn Langan pose in the yard of their Encino, California, home. *(Ginny Benjamin)*

In 1962 Barrymore starred in the European-made picture *The Pharoah's Woman*.

JOHN BARRYMORE, JR.

The scion of two famous theatrical families was born on June 4, 1932, in Beverly Hills. When he was eighteen months old his mother, Dolores Costello,[2] the daughter of matinee idol Maurice Costello and a movie star in her own right, separated from his father, John Barrymore. When John, Jr., was seven years old she married the doctor who had delivered him.

Barrymore received no encouragement to act from his father who he recalls seeing only once, Christmas Eve, 1939. His mother was definitely against his becoming an actor. But he had inherited the famous name and profile. The question was whether he had the talent and temperament as well.

His film debut *The Sundowners* (1950) brought respectable notices. Subsequently what was said about him on the entertainment pages was lost in the headlines his behavior produced. In 1951 he withdrew at the last minute from two plays in a row. The next year he married actress Cara Williams. One of their frequent quarrels landed him in jail and after their divorce she took him to court for nonpayment of alimony and support of their son John III.

In 1957 he reacted to a one-year suspension by Actors Equity by suing the union. He threatened to sue the producers of Diana Barrymore's autobiography *Too Much, Too Soon*. During the same period he was arrested at different times for speeding, hit and run driving, and drunkenness.

During the four years he spent in Rome in the early sixties he made 16 features and had almost as many run-ins with the law. One was when he broke into a starlet's apartment to retrieve his engagement ring. Then there was a street fistfight, a quarrel with the police, and frequent break-ups and make-ups with his second wife, an Italian actress.

He returned to Hollywood in 1964 and told Hedda Hopper he would write screen plays. Instead he sued a producer for dubbing his voice in *The Christine Keeler Story* (1964), rammed his auto into a police car, walked out on the lead role of a network TV series, was questioned by the F.B.I. about a bomb hoax, and was arrested for leaving the scene of an accident and several times for possession of marijuana. He served one jail sentence of 60 days.

Somehow he managed to sandwich in some movies: *Quebec* (1951), *Thunderbirds* (1952), and *High School Confidential!* (1958).

The last few years Barrymore has spent completely alone in a shack in the California desert fasting and meditating. He did one *Kung Fu* TV episode in 1974 as a favor to his very close friend David Carradine. Not only has he stopped drinking but he claims to be a yoga, vegetarian, and celibate. In his solitude he told an interviewer, "I have found God and myself. It is pure bliss."

John leads a very different life today.

Archie, who called himself the "Ole Mongoose," won the Light Heavyweight Championship of the World on December 17, 1952.

ARCHIE MOORE

The boxer who held the Light Heavyweight Championship from 1952 to 1961 was born Archibald Lee Wright in Benoit, Mississippi, on December 13, 1913. Before he had his first professional fight in 1936 Archie had been toughened up in a reform school for stealing a few dollars from the fare box of a streetcar.

During the sixteen years between his ring debut and attaining the crown Moore fought 169 bouts. He was defeated 22 times (three times at the hands of Ezzard Charles [2]) but knocked out 106 opponents.

Archie relieved Joey Maxim of his Light Heavyweight crown in 15 rounds on December 17, 1952. Maxim met with Moore twice after that but both times was defeated. Bobo Olson was KO'd by Archie when he challenged his championship in 1956.

Moore was thirty-nine years old when he won the title, an age when most boxers are considered to be washed-up.

In his two attempts to become Heavyweight Champion Archie was knocked out by Rocky Marciano in 1955 and Floyd Patterson a year later.

In 1960 the National Boxing Association withdrew their recognition of his crown when they could not agree with his managers about forthcoming matches. In a similar dispute in 1962 both the European and New York associations refused to acknowledge him as champ.

Archie fought once more after Muhammad Ali knocked him out in the fourth round on November 15, 1962. He flattened Mike Di Biase and called it quits.

His ring career over, Moore made his colorful personality work for him reading poetry on college campuses, running for political office twice (both times unsuccessfully), and writing books, *The Archie Moore Story* (1960) and *Any Boy Can* (1971).

For a time he had a training camp in the hills near San Diego. Muhammad Ali was one of his guests but only briefly. The two did not see eye to eye. His last boxing job was as adviser to George Foreman when he took the Heavyweight title from Joe Frazier in 1973.

Moore's success with delinquents rivals even his record in the ring. His "A B C" (Any Boy Can) program is credited with dramatically reducing crime and vandalism in his area. In 1968 his city named him "Mr. San Diego."

Archie and his wife live in a huge home with a bar, pool table, and swimming pool all shaped like boxing gloves. His fourth marriage has produced five children plus two more the Moores have adopted.

Archie and his daughter Reena in the yard of their home in San Diego. *(Jason Keith McCormick)*

In 1937 June was under contract to Twentieth Century-Fox, a studio known for beautiful blondes.

JUNE LANG

The luscious, blue-eyed blonde was born June Vlasek on May 5 in Minneapolis, Minnesota. By the time her family moved to Los Angeles when she was seven years old she had already been dancing professionally for two years.

In Hollywood she performed as a Meglin Kiddie at local vaudeville houses and in her teens began dancing in the chorus line. She worked as an extra in *Young Sinners* (1931) with Dorothy Jordan (the widow of Meriam C. Cooper living in Coronado) before getting a bit part in *She Wanted a Millionaire* (1932). The director took a liking to her and she was put under contract. The Fox studio production chief Winifield Sheehan took a personal interest and had her teeth straightened. She was in *Music in the Air* (1934) and there was talk that she was the threat to Marian Nixon (married to Ben Lyon [4]).

In 1935 Sheehan was out at Fox and so was June. But within a few months the same studio's new casting director spotted her dancing at the Trocadero. She was not only signed again but Darryl F. Zanuck who took over Sheehan's job shared his predecessor's enthusiasm for her potential. Although her parts were sometimes awkward she was always photographed lovingly. Surrounded by the world's most beautiful people June still stood out. They cast her in the unlikely roles of Warner Baxter's girl friend in *The Road to Glory* (1936) and as Shirley Temple's mother in *Wee Willie Winkie* (1937). Then she supported Eddie Cantor in *Ali Baba Goes to Town* (1937).

From the build-up she was being given it was obvious that Fox was grooming her for big things. Then in 1938 while in London to make a film she was panicked by the Munich crisis and left. Her contract was cancelled. Hal Roach used her in *Captain Fury* (1939) and she was in *Red Head* (1941) and *Flesh and Fantasy* (1943) but everything she did after Fox was either a small part or a small picture. She was persona non grata at all the major lots.

Her brief, disastrous marriage to convicted hoodlum Johnny Roselli, who was a crony of the late Frank Costello, did her career no good either. Before that she had been wed to agent Vic Orsatti.

Her last pictures, *Three of a Kind* (1944) and *Lighthouse* (1946), were cheapies.

From 1944 to 1954 June was married to a businessman. Their bitter, messy divorce was well reported by the press.

June lives in a small, very neat house in North Hollywood. Her biggest disappointment in recent years came when her only child Patricia preferred working with retarded children to a movie contract. "I don't understand people today," she told an interviewer. "I don't like these times and I do not wish to be part of them." She sees no one from her Hollywood days and none of her neighbors know she has been in pictures. June does not like modern movies or the people who make them. She feels their long hair and beards probably affect their work.

June in her North Hollywood home with actor-friend Kirk Crivello. *(Claude Wagner)*

Jean's son Aric and her daughter Patricia posed with her in this 1954 M-G-M publicity still.

JEAN HAGEN

The versatile actress of films, stage, and TV was born Jean Shirley Verhagen in Chicago on August 3, 1925. She put herself through Northwestern University with money she earned acting on radio shows such as *That Brewster Boy.*

She came to New York City in late 1945 and got a job ushering in a Broadway theatre where Charles MacArthur and Ben Hecht's play *Swan Song* was in rehearsal. At a cast party the authors overheard her deriding their play and instead of firing her Jean was auditioned for one of the roles. She got the part but the play closed after a very short run.

Her next break was in Lillian Hellman's *Another Part of the Forest* (1946). After that she did *Ghosts* (1948). Producer Sam Zimbalist and director Anthony Mann caught her in *The Traitor* (1949) one night and gave her a screen test the following morning. Within days she was put under contract to M-G-M and in the cast of the film *Side Street* (1950).

Jean Hagen accomplished something that very few ever achieve. She played almost every conceivable type of role on the screen. She was a dipso singer in *Side Street*, a frontier woman in *Carbine Williams* (1952), Red Skelton's wife in *Half a Hero* (1953), a memorable tramp in *The Big*

Knife (1955), Betty Hutton's best friend in *Spring Reunion* (1957), F.D.R.'s secretary in *Sunrise at Campobello* (1960), and a supercilious matron in her last film *Dead Ringer* (1964). She was more than convincing in all of them but in the final analysis the range of her talents worked against her. She had no "image" and it automatically killed her chances of having the studio build her into a star.

When she played the screechy voiced silent star in *Singin' in the Rain* (1952) she all but stole the picture and won an Oscar nomination. But much of the public who noticed her as the pathetic gangster's girl in *Asphalt Jungle* (1950) never realized she was the same actress.

She was the mother on *Make Room for Daddy* for three seasons beginning in 1953. Jean played fourth fiddle to Danny Thomas and his fictitious son and daughter. The only reason she accepted the part was because she was given 7 percent of the series. She did the most she could with a generally thankless role and was nominated for an Emmy in both 1954 and 1955.

Jean has been divorced since 1965 and has been quite ill most of the time since. Her room at the Motion Picture Country Hospital is filled with books, photos of her two children, and stuffed animals. Asked about future plans she replied: "Acting is all I've wanted to do since I was a kid growing up in Elkhart, Illinois. I want more than anything else to work again and with the help of God I will."

Jean has been living for the past few years at the Motion Picture Country Hospital. *(Jerry Goodman)*

August 23, 1948, was the twenty-second anniversary of the death of the great lover of the silent screen and Ditra's visit to his tomb was well covered by the press. (*Wide World Photo*)

DITRA FLAMÈ
"THE LADY IN BLACK"

The mysterious figure who appeared annually at the tomb of Rudolph Valentino was born Ditra Helena Mefford on August 4, 1905, in Los Angeles. Throughout her childhood Ditra was both overweight and sickly.

According to Ditra she first met Valentino in 1919. He had not yet made a name in movies. She admits to having had a "bobby soxer's crush" on him. He liked her, she says, but in no way led her on. His name for her was "Sorellina" which in Italian means "little sister."

As Valentino's career caught fire the two remained friends. She was also in show business under the name Ditra Flamè as part of an all-girl band. Later she danced in vaudeville in an act called "The Tiny Tots Revue," a group of fat girls similar to the famous "Beef Trust."

In 1920 Valentino visited her in the hospital where she was undergoing a mastoid operation. When she told him she was afraid she was going to die he replied that he felt she would live for many years more. To comfort her he added that whoever of the two survived should visit the other's grave with flowers.

At 12:10 P.M. on August 23, 1926, the great lover of the silent screen died in New York City.

There is no record of Ditra visiting his tomb in Hollywood Memorial Park Cemetery until the 1940s. Many have laid claim to being the original "Lady in Black," including Marian Benda, who was equally well publicized until her recent suicide. It has also been said that "The Lady in Black" was nothing more than a publicity stunt arranged annually by Hollywood press agents. This accusation pains Ditra most of all. She says the very reason she stopped making her appearances after 1954 was that she hated the publicity. Another reason is that Valentino's family had threatened her with legal action if the dramatic visits did not cease.

On the twenty-fifth anniversary of his death Ditra fainted. While unconscious she had, she says, a vision. When revived she knew that her real mission in life was spreading the word of God. Until then Ditra had sung blues on the radio, ran a music studio, and staged Valentino shows. In 1928 she had walked to New York City to lose weight. After 1954, her last public appearance at the tomb, she began leading street revival meetings and then spent six years as an evangelist at an Indian rescue mission in Arizona.

She has never been married and says all of her boyfriends have been dark and handsome. "I guess," says Ditra laughingly, "you could say that I always dug the Latin types."

Now she lives alongside a railroad track in a frame building that houses her Pentecostal Church and a cat refuge. She has several letters from her legendary friend and a locket he gave her many years ago.

For years Ditra refused even to divulge her name but in a recent interview she told even how the famous black dress and veil came into being: "I was always such a fatty that I felt black slimmed me down. I still wear it all the time."

"The Lady in Black" after an interview with the author's associate Martitia Palmer. *(Jeannie Youngson)*

The publicity that Mickey reveled in finally caught up with him.

MICKEY COHEN

The gambler whom Senator Estes Kefauver once called "a contemptible little mobster" was born Meyer Harris Cohen in Brooklyn on September 4, 1913. He was a chronic truant and troublemaker in the Boyle Heights area of Los Angeles where he grew up. Arrested at nine years of age for bootlegging, Mickey quit grammar school and began fighting other newsboys for the choice streetcorners downtown.

He ended his mediocre boxing career after 79 matches in 1934 and pleaded guilty shortly thereafter to a charge of armed robbery.

In 1939 he returned to Los Angeles as the protégé of racketeer Jake "Greasy Thumb" Guzik. Mickey was a minor underworld figure conspicuous mainly for his cockiness and zooty clothes until, in 1947, he took over as the gambling czar of the West Coast after "Bugsy" Siegel was murdered. Cohen relished the limelight and became as much of a celebrity as the movie stars he hobnobbed with.

He spent from 1951 to 1955 in prison for tax evasion but never lost control of the more than 10,000 bookies under him. At his height he reportedly handled $600,000 a day in bets. There have been over a dozen attempts on his life. One in 1950 was a dynamite blast that blew out the front of his expensive home. Five years earlier when Maxie Shaman, whom Cohen refers to as "a welsher," pulled a gun on him, Mickey shot and killed him. But his real enemy was the late Los Angeles Police Chief William Parker. During a 1957 TV interview Cohen referred to him as "a sadistic degenerate" and "known alcoholic." The remarks cost the network a public apology and a $45,000 settlement.

96

He dated stripper Candy Barr (serving a sentence in a Texas prison) and Miss Beverly Hills. Johnny Stompanato financed his fling with Lana Turner on money he borrowed from Mickey. After Cheryl Crane [3] killed him it was Cohen who paid for the funeral. Unreported in the press at the time were many generous and thoughtful kindnesses Cohen carried out without any fanfare. William Randolph Hearst, Sr., ordered his papers to stop referring to Cohen as a "gangster" when some of these acts were made known to him.

It all came to an end for Mickey when he was sent to Alcatraz in 1961 for his second prison term on a count of attempted tax evasion. His only bitterness for the 11 years he spent behind bars is reserved for Bobby Kennedy whom he recently called "a punk who never knew what hunger was." He won a $125,000 judgment, which the I.R.S. confiscated, when he was beaten almost to death by another inmate.

A greatly subdued Mickey lives alone in a luxuriously furnished Brentwood apartment. He walks with the aid of two canes and has daily therapy. He still does not drink, smoke, or swear. Two other characteristics that have never left him are his passion for ice cream and his obsession with germs. Every day one of his sisters looks in on him with homemade cookies or soup.

Cohen, who is still on parole, is a friend and enthusiast of Billy Graham but still considers himself a Jew.

Asked recently if the four years he spent in solitary was the worst aspect of his confinement he replied: "No. The most degrading part of jail for me was having to be close to homosexuals and other degenerate elements."

Mickey lives alone today in an apartment in West Los Angeles. *(Ginny Benjamin)*

Florence beat Gertrude Ederle's 1926 record by one hour and eleven minutes when she swam the Channel on August 8, 1950. *(A.P. Photo)*

FLORENCE CHADWICK

The first woman to swim the English Channel four times and to break the speed record of Gertrude Ederle was born in San Diego on November 9, 1918. Her uncle taught her to swim when she was five years old. At age six she entered her first contest and came in last. Says Florence, "I can still remember the humiliation I felt but it only made me want to win more than ever."

One year later in her second swim meet she came in next to last. But when she was ten Florence heard of Gertrude Ederle, who two years before had become the first woman to swim the English Channel. After that Miss Ederle was her heroine and the Channel was her life goal.

The next year Florence won a race swimming the San Diego Bay. She was the first child to do it and during the next eighteen years she was seven times the winner of the annual two and a half mile race.

Florence prepared for her Channel swim while working for an American oil firm in Saudi Arabia. She saved the $5,000 needed and trained in the Persian Gulf.

On August 8, 1950, at 2:37 A.M. she entered the cold choppy waters off the French coast at Cape Gris Nez. When she touched the English shore after 13 hours and 20 minutes she had set a new world's record for women.

The other three times she swam the Channel (in 1951, 1953, and 1955) she began from the English side, which is considered the easier route. She was the first woman to swim both ways.

She failed twice to swim the Irish Sea from Ireland to Scotland. Only one man has ever succeeded in the treacherous waters. In 1955 she had to desert the icy currents of Juan de Fuca in Canada. Florence admits that all three of the tries were great disappointments to her.

Her home town gave her a ticker-tape parade and a white, purple-tipped dahlia was named for her.

Florence made the most of her fame and success. She became an adviser to Catalina Swimwear and was Aquatic Director of Grossinger's. There were Florence Chadwick Swimming Schools in New York, New Jersey, and California. For many years she was the world's highest-paid woman athlete, averaging as much as $2,500 weekly.

She is now advising and training a young San Diego woman who will soon attempt to conquer the Channel.

Florence seldom swims anymore "except in the sea of finance," she says with a laugh. She is a stockbroker with the firm of Kidder, Peabody & Co. in San Diego.

She and Gertrude Ederle [1] still exchange notes and cards each Christmas.

Florence is a stockbroker with Kidder, Peabody & Co. in San Diego. *(Ene Riisna)*

Betty got star billing in burlesque houses from coast to coast as the "Ball of Fire."

BETTY ROWLAND

Burlesque's "Ball of Fire" was born Betty Jane Rowland in Columbus, Ohio, on January 23. Betty and her two sisters took dancing lessons from a very early age. After appearing locally in talent shows Diann and Betty Rowland began touring in vaudeville as a sister act.

When the Depression hit the Rowlands were out of a job for several months until an agent got them into the chorus line of the famous Old Howard Theatre in Boston. The year was 1932. At first they did their specialty act and kept their clothes on. But after a short time they went on as singles and both became strippers.

For their parents it seemed the end of the world. Their father was a probation officer who was so strict that he refused to allow his wife to wear a bathing suit on a public beach. "But he soon came around," said Betty recently. "Dad ended up keeping scrapbooks on all three of us girls."

Her older sister Diann was appearing in a Detroit nightclub when she died of a heart condition in 1945. The youngest Rowland, Rozelle, became a burlesque star in her own right and was billed as "The Golden Girl." She is now married to a titled Belgian and is known as the Baroness Empain. She and her wealthy husband have homes in Paris and New York.

Betty was shorter than most of the queens of the runway and found that moving her body in 6/8 time made her seem taller. A less accomplished dancer would have been simply vulgar but Betty moved not only quickly but very gracefully and her clothes fell by the wayside very slowly. Her musical theme was "In the Mood." Reviewers compared her to a whirling dervish. Not only were her features very pretty and her proportions generous but she had skin like satin.

Orson Welles, whom she used to date, offered her a dramatic role in the stage production *Five Kings* but Betty passed it up. She loved burlesque and has no regrets. At the time she was making $2,000 a week peeling.

Betty gave it all up in 1951 for marriage to a wealthy lumberman. They shared a Bel-Aire mansion until their divorce in 1964.

She now lives with her poodle in a garden apartment of a luxury building in Brentwood. Betty still sees her contemporary Margie Hart (living in the Trusdale Estates of Beverly Hills) and many of her old fans. They drop in to see her at a bar only blocks away from the ocean in Santa Monica. Betty works there several nights a week as a bartender. She doesn't need the money but admits that the attention paid her is pleasing. "I don't miss burlesque the way it is now but I think about the good old days a lot. The kids stripping today don't know what a wonderful business it was." If the management requests it and the mood strikes her, the "Ball of Fire" will still strip.

The "Ball of Fire" lives in a Brentwood apartment with her poodle. *(Shelly Davis)*

Ray Noble's droll wit as well as his music made him a great favorite on radio in the late thirties and forties. *(National Broadcasting Company)*

RAY NOBLE

The orchestra leader-composer-radio personality was born in Hove, England, on December 17, 1903. He had had several years of piano lessons even before his family moved to London in 1912.

For a while Ray led a small band and then went with a publisher as an arranger of dance music. The BBC hired him to be their house band arranger. Then in 1929 he joined the HMV label (RCA Victor in England) where he assembled the all-star New Mayfair Orchestra. According to Noble it was put together "to record all the songs no one else would do." Due chiefly to his arrangements his records did extremely well not only in England but also in the United States.

He arrived in the United States in late 1934 and worked briefly at Paramount on a musical which was never produced. When Ray returned to New York to form an orchestra, the studio permitted him to take one of his compositions with him. The one he chose, "The Touch of Your Lips," became a hit.

Glenn Miller assisted Noble in forming his aggregation and played second trombone for him. Charlie Spivak was on first trombone. Wil Bradley and Claude Thornhill were also members of his original group.

Along with tours and one-nighters the Ray Noble Orchestra's main stand was the Rainbow Room on top of Rockefeller Center. It was there he first worked with Edgar Bergen [2] and Charlie McCarthy.

He moved to Hollywood in the late thirties and began making a name for himself on the radio variety show headed by George Burns and Gracie Allen. Although most of the material he used was written for him, the radio personality which developed was strictly his own creation. The character he played with Burns and Allen and later on the *Chase and Sanborn Hour* was very much like P. G. Wodehouse's "Bertie Wooster" and very unlike the real Noble.

Noble was in a few movies, *Damsel in Distress* (1937) and *Here We Go Again* (1942) but radio was really his medium. Musicologist George Simon described the Noble sound thusly: "For sheer good taste and all-around smart dance music, that was the band of the times." His opening and closing themes, both his own compositions, were hits then and are now considered standards: "The Very Thought of You" and "Good Night, Sweetheart." Another of his big ones departed totally from the smooth, sweet sound for which he was best known—"Cherokee."

For all his success Noble had no trouble in walking away from his career in 1955. He and his wife (who are childless) settled for ten years on the Isle of Jersey off the coast of England. Now they are based in Santa Barbara but travel about six months of the year.

He is very pleased about the renewed interest in his type of music and flattered that he is so well remembered. But nothing could induce him to return. Today his interests are gardening and listening to records—not his own. "I'm afraid, old boy," said Noble to a visitor recently, "that I have become a classical music buff."

Ray now makes his home in Santa Barbara when he and his wife are not traveling. *(Zena La Vey)*

Gale's first TV series, *My Little Margie,* premiered over the CBS network on June 16, 1952.

GALE STORM

The TV star of the 1950s was born Josephine Owaissa Cottle on April 5, 1921, in Bloomington, Texas. Her father died when she was seventeen months old.

In 1939 Gale was the winner of Jesse Lasky's "Gateway to Hollywood" talent search. She was put under contract to RKO Pictures but was dropped after only six months. She went next to Monogram and then to Universal.

Gale made very little impact in movies. In addition to appearing in several westerns as Roy Rogers's leading lady she made: *Tom Brown's School Days* (1940) with Freddie Bartholomew,[1] *Where Are Your Children?* (1943) with Patricia Morrison (single and living in Park La Brea Towers in Los Angeles), *The Underworld Story* (1950) with the late Dan Duryea, *The Kid From Texas* (1950) with the late Audie Murphy, and *Woman of the North Country* (1952) with Ruth Hussey [4] and Rod Cameron (living in Malibu, California).

Gale's first television series, *My Little Margie,* was one of the most popular situation comedies on the networks from 1952 to 1955. It is still being syndicated around the world. Her costar was Charles Farrell [2] who played her father. After filming 126 of the thirty-minute episodes she had her second hit with *Oh, Susanna.* It survived for three seasons in prime time beginning in 1956. Slapstick and improbable situations were the mainstays of the plots of both. Occasionally Gale would sing.

In 1955 her record of "I Hear You Knocking" was for a while the second most popular disc in the nation. The same year the Gale Storm rendition of "Teen-Age Prayer" was on the hit charts for 15 weeks straight. Two years later her "Dark Moon" was on Billboard's Top 100 list for 23 weeks. She has sold over four million records.

Since 1941 Gale has been married to Lee Bonnell who for a time acted under the name of Terry Belmont. He now owns an insurance agency near the Bonnell's home in Encino, California. They have three boys and a girl. Gale's youngest, Susanna, was named for her television show. The Bonnells have been grandparents for several years.

Her appearances on TV since her shows went off the air have been very scarce. Because of re-runs seen around the country she can still command a sizeable fee for dinner theatre productions of such shows as *Cactus Flower* and *The Unsinkable Molly Brown*. Although she has no financial need to work again Gale by no means considers herself retired and greatly resents being considered a has-been.

Gale and her businessman husband attend a recent Hollywood gala. *(Frank Edwards)*

Jeffrey Lynn's career got a big boost from his part in *Four Daughters* (1938).

JEFFREY LYNN

The popular young leading man was born Ragnar Godfrey Lind on February 16, 1909, in Auburn, Massachusetts. While getting his teaching degree at Bates College and later as a drama and English instructor in a high school he found himself drawn into little theatre groups. After a year of teaching he moved to New York City and supported himself as an usher in a newsreel theatre while he made the rounds of casting offices. Jeffrey first acted in stock and then began to land small roles in Broadway plays such as *A Slight Case of Murder* (1935). He toured for six months with Walter Hampton in *Cyrano de Bergerac* (1936). When he got the lead in the road company of *Brother Rat* (1936) he was working at Macy's. M-G-M tested Lynn but it was Warner Brothers who put him under contract in 1937.

He was in *Cowboy from Brooklyn* (1938) with Dick Foran (living in Van Nuys, California), *Yes, My Darling Daughter* (1939), *The Roaring Twenties* (1939), *The Fighting 69th* (1940), and *Flight from Destiny* (1941) with Mona Maris (living in South America).

After spending World War II as a Captain in Army Intelligence he resumed his career in *Black Bart* (1948), *A Letter to Three Wives* (1949), and *Captain China* (1950). It is however the series that began with *Four Daughters* (1938) which brought him the most recognition. Although he has not heard from Priscilla Lane in many years he is fondly remembered as her beau in four features.

During the fifties and early sixties he was busy on TV dramatic shows and touring in plays such as *The Caine Mutiny Court Martial* and *Philadelphia Story*. He played the title role in the national company of *Mister Roberts* and toured as late as 1959 in *Two for the Seasaw*. His last film credits are *Butterfield 8* (1960) and *Tony Rome* (1967).

Jeffrey Lynn had three chances for stardom. He tested with Paulette Goddard [1] for the role of Ashley in *Gone With the Wind* but didn't get it. The producer and writer wanted him for *The Devil and Miss Jones* but Jack Warner refused to loan him and Bob Cummings was used. Shortly afterward when that film's director Sam Wood was assigned to *Kings Row* he adamantly refused Warner's insistence that Lynn play in it and Cummings was hired at a large fee. The last opportunity, which Lynn admits was entirely his own doing, was when he chose to honor a verbal agreement to play a short run in the Midwest and therefore had to forego taking over the lead from John Forsyth in *The Teahouse of the August Moon* on Broadway.

He would like to act again but despairs over the changes in the movie business and the world in general. He has two grown children by his first wife, Robin Chandler, who is now married to diplomat Angier Biddle Duke. Jeffrey is now married to a woman over twenty years his junior and is the adoptive father of her seven children. They share a house in Tarzana, California, with two dogs, two cats, and tropical fish. Lynn supports his brood with a full-time job with a product testing firm and a night job as a manager of a neighborhood movie theatre.

Jeffrey with Ann Lee, one of his seven adopted children. *(Richard Joseph Davis)*

In 1945 Beatrice appeared in the movie version of *Billy Rose's Diamond Horseshoe*.

BEATRICE KAY

The singer-actress who came into her own during the Gay Nineties craze of the 1940s was born Beatrice Kupper on April 21 in New York City. She is the great-grandniece of unionist Samuel Gompers and two of her aunts were well-known theatrical costumers.

She debuted at age six as *Little Lord Fauntleroy* in Colonel McCauley's Stock Company in Louisville, Kentucky. As a child Beatrice doubled for Madge Evans in some silent pictures and became known in vaudeville as "the miniature mimic." Her other specialty was doing her songs in a variety of dialects.

As a teenager she was billed for a while as Honey Kay. She was seen on Broadway in such shows as *What's in a Name?* (1920), *Secrets* (1922), and *Rain or Shine* (1928).

Work was scarce during the Depression. By 1938 she was singing in the *Provincetown Follies* when she developed a severe case of laryngitis. She was strongly advised to rest her vocal cords for at least a year. Instead she continued performing and developed an odd, raspy quality to her voice. The drastic change killed any chance she ever had to achieve her goal—light opera. It did however open up a whole new career to her.

When she auditioned for Billy Rose's nitery, the Diamond Horseshoe, singing the raucous "Ta Ra Ra Boom De Ay" she was hired on the spot. When she left Rose seventeen months later she had sung the song 1,190 times—two shows a night, seven nights a week. She had been poorly paid for her efforts but was now a very hot property.

By listening to old cylinders of the Gay Nineties Bea mastered the technique of the period perfectly. *The Beatrice Kay Show* replaced Fred Allen's radio program one summer and then she was signed by Model Tobacco for their *Gay 90s Revue*. The highly successful Monday night radio series was heard over CBS during the 1940–41 and 1941–42 seasons. She became the only living artist associated with songs of the turn of the century and has managed to make a good living ever since. Her recordings for Columbia sold very well and she had a program for a while over WOR in New York City.

Beatrice is somewhat cynical about her career and regrets that her devotion to it broke up her marriages to "some very nice men." Then too the potential many saw in her as an actress was never realized. Her performance in the film *Underworld, U.S.A.* (1961) was outstanding. She impressed everyone who saw her in *A Time for Dying* but it was never shown in this country.

She is still singing songs like "Only a Bird in a Gilded Cage" and "Don't Go in the Lion's Cage Tonight" at Santa Monica's Mayfair Music Hall where she is house soubrette.

Her mother died in 1972 at 94 and Beatrice now lives with her poodle. She is especially contemptuous of Hollywood. "I've lived here fourteen years," she told an interviewer recently, "and have only two people who I could really call friends in the whole damn town."

Beatrice and her constant companion, Bippy. *(Peter Schaeffer)*

Les Tremayne and Barbara Luddy in a 1941 publicity still.

By 1944 Olan Soulé had taken over as Barbara Luddy's leading man. (*Maurice Seymour*)

THE FIRST NIGHTER

The longest running, best remembered, and most popular radio playhouse premiered at 8:00 P.M. on Thanksgiving night 1930. It was created to advertise a hand lotion, Campana's Italian Balm (the "Italian" was dropped from its name during World War II). Its theme for over twenty-two years was "Neapolitan Nights."

Each week a thirty-minute, two-act play was presented from the fictional "Little Theatre off Times Square." The debonaire host would alight from his taxi to be greeted each week by the ticket-taker's salutation, "Good evening, Mr. First Nighter. The usher will show you to your seat." Scanning the program Mr. First Nighter would mention the play's title, author, cast, and whether it was to be a romance, comedy, drama, or mystery.

Its only challenger for popularity was the *Lux Radio Theatre* which did not begin until years later and had the advantages of a huge budget, a full hour of air time, and used the most famous properties and stars in Hollywood. Still *Lux* never did more than tie *The First Nighter* for first place in the polls.

No one who remembers the heyday of radio can forget the page's call at intermissions, "Smoking in the downstairs and outer lobby only, please!" The role was played by Harry Elders and Gil Stratton, Jr. (now a TV sportcaster in Los Angeles).

The original Mr. First Nighter was Charles Hughes. Others were: Francis X. Bushman, Ed Prentiss, Marvin Miller, MacDonald Carey, and Brett Morrison.

The leads were played first by Jack Doty and June Meredith. Doty died and Miss Meredith left shortly after the show began. Don Ameche and Betty Lou Gerson (living in Los Angeles) played the parts until Barbara Luddy and Les Tremayne took over in June of 1937. Tremayne was replaced in 1943 by Olan Soulé who was Miss Luddy's leading man until the final curtain fell in the summer of 1953. Tremayne and Soulé had both played Coach Hardy on *Jack Armstrong*.[4] Soulé was also Ah Ha, the Chinese cook on *Little Orphan Annie*. Tremayne was the leading man on radio's *Grand Hotel*. Both men live in Los Angeles and work constantly. Soulé is the voice of Batman on the animated TV series. Miss Luddy, who is as close to a star as radio ever produced, lives in the San Fernando Valley. Because of failing eyesight she is inactive.

The show used only original scripts. The actors wore formal clothes and did the broadcasts before a live audience. Once a man in the front row dropped dead during a comedy. Neither cigarettes or alcohol were ever mentioned. Once the word "darn" was used and brought many strong complaints.

Although the most they ever made was a relatively meager $350 a broadcast, when they met recently Tremayne said, "I've been in forty movies and a hit Broadway play but *The First Nighter* was the greatest thing that ever happened to me." Soulé and Luddy heartily agreed.

Along with excellent direction by the late Joe Ainley the quality that the program had that held its audience so long and still triggers so many fond memories was the atmosphere it simulated—Broadway, The Great White Way on an opening night! For most of its listeners that was something they would only know via this series. Ironically, *The First Nighter* emanated from Chicago and then from Hollywood—never New York. Barbara Luddy has never even been to New York City.

Olan Soulé, Barbara Luddy, and Les Tremayne in a recent and rare reunion. *(Ivan Cury)*

In 1956 the U.S. Lawn Tennis Association named May Sutton Bundy to their Tennis Hall of Fame. *(World Wide Photo)*

MAY SUTTON BUNDY

The grand dowager of tennis was born in Plymouth, England, on September 25, 1887. When she was six years old she came to Southern California on her father's sailboat and was raised on a ranch in Pasadena.

The first the public knew the name May Sutton was when at the age of thirteen she won the Southern California Women's Championship in 1900. Then in 1904, at the age of seventeen, on her first appearance at the U. S. National Championships she took the Women's Singles without the loss of a set.

In the same year, she became the first American to win at Wimbledon. England was just getting over the shock when she did it again in 1907. On New Year's Day 1908 May was the Queen of the Tournament of Roses.

Her whole life has been tennis. In 1912 she married the late Thomas Bundy. He and Maurice McLoughlin won the National Men's Doubles from 1912 to 1914. Their daughter Dorothy Cheney won 11 straight Women's Hard Court Singles titles between 1957 and 1967. Like her mother she is active in tennis promotion in Los Angeles. May's sisters Adele and

Florence, ages 101 and 91 respectively, are no longer playing but remain ardent fans. At one time they too were so good there was a saying, "It takes a Sutton to beat a Sutton."

Mrs. Bundy left the courts for a while to raise her family. When she came back in 1921 she still ranked fourth in the country. As late as 1928 she was rated fifth in the nation at the age of 41. That was the year she returned to Wimbledon and went to the singles semi-finals before losing. She then turned professional in 1930 and devoted the next 34 years of her life to teaching the game.

She rates Helen Wills Moody [1] as the best woman player ever. The only time they played Mrs. Bundy lost to her. "But," she says, "that was after I had had four children."

The matriarch lives alone in a cottage in the Santa Monica Canyon surrounded by flowers. Not only does the octogenarian drive her own car and tend her garden but she still plays tennis often (still with a wooden racket). Or as she says, "Whenever I can get someone to play an old lady."

It was in defeat, not victory, that May Sutton Bundy earned her real immortality with tennis fans. At Forest Hills in 1930 she was within a point of victory over Hazel Hotchkiss Wightman in the National Championships when she fractured her left leg and dislocated her right elbow. She shifted her racket to her left hand, borrowed a crutch, and finished the match in order not to default and rob Mrs. Wightman of a victory. The *Book of American Lawn Tennis* said of it: "This match demonstrated what was probably the finest display of courage, good sportsmanship, fighting spirit and the will to win ever exhibited in the history of tennis."

Ms. Bundy still plays with a wooden racket. *(Linda Harkavy)*

In 1945 Louis was in the picture
And Then There Were None.

LOUIS HAYWARD

The stage and movie actor was born on March 19, 1909, in Johannesburg, South Africa. Just before Louis was born his father, who was a mining engineer, was killed. His mother brought him up mainly in London. He spent several years in a Jesuit school in Brittany. For a while he was an acting pupil in London along with Laurence Olivier. He showed so little promise that his mother received a note from the head of the school informing her that Louis was wasting his time and her money.

Soon after he began getting breaks on the London stage he clicked as a handsome young leading man. Noel Coward chose him for *Conversation Piece* opposite Yvonne Printemps. He played a lunatic in the West End production of *Dracula* and was with Constance Collier in *Hay Fever*. When he did *Another Language* with Edna Best and the late Herbert Marshall his understudy was the unknown Rex Harrison.

Hayward's appearance on Broadway with the Lunts in *Point Valaine* (1935) got him an M-G-M contract. He was cast in a succession of mediocre pictures with the exception of *Anthony Adverse* (1936). Then when the iceskater Jack Dunn was killed the title role of *The Duke of West Point* (1938) went to Louis.

For the next fifteen years he was very much in demand. He played the suave detective The Saint in a series of features and was one of the screen's leading swashbucklers in such films as *The Son of Monte Cristo* (1940), *The Pirates of Capri* (1949), and *Captain Pirate* (1952). His best performance was in *Ladies in Retirement* (1941) as one of the most thoroughly amoral and hateful characters in fiction. Playing his aunt in the picture was Ida Lupino, who was his wife at the time.

During World War II Louis won a Bronze Star as an officer in the Marine Corps. It was a Marine photographic unit under his direction that filmed the Battle of Tarawa.

As early as 1949 Hayward was getting a percentage of the profits of his films. He lived in Italy for a while where he turned out a string of costume epics. He had an interest in *The Lone Wolf* television series of the early fifties in which he also starred. His later series *The Pursuers* was not a success.

Illness made him withdraw from the touring company of *Camelot* in 1963. Although he is now in good health he has remained mostly inactive.

The one disappointment of his career was that he never played in Shakespeare. With a humility never shown in his performances he admitted recently, "I expect I could have managed to get a part but the truth is that I just wasn't up to playing it."

Louis never socialized much with the Hollywood set even in his heyday. He and his third wife now live in Palm Springs but they see very little of the movie colony there.

After making over forty features he is still recognized all over the world from the title role in an adventure movie he made in 1939. "I used to resent it," says an amused Hayward, "but I've come around to enjoying the experience. Wherever I go there's someone pointing a finger at me exclaiming 'Look, there's *The Man in the Iron Mask!*' "

Louis lives now in Palm Springs. *(Michael Knowles)*

Ethel Merman (left) played Perle (right) in *Call Me Madam,* the Broadway and movie musical. *(U.P.I.)*

PERLE MESTA

The Washington party giver who was immortalized in song by Irving Berlin as "the hostess with the mostess on the ball" was born Perle Skirvin in Sturgis, Michigan. Her father had made millions in Texas oil and Oklahoma real estate and her husband was a wealthy industrialist.

Perle began entertaining in the nation's capital during World War I. She was a generous contributor to Republican coffers and a frequent guest at the White House as far back as President Coolidge's term.

She has been a widow since 1925. One of her big romances is said to have been with Herbert Hoover's Vice-President, Charles Curtis.

Perle was a staunch Republican until 1940. Before then she was known only in Washington circles. She came into her own as a Democrat and an early champion of Harry S. Truman. She gave Margaret Truman her coming-out party and when the President's daughter sang in Oklahoma City Perle gave a party for her that is legend in that part of the country. In 1948 and 1949 she was co-chairperson of the Jefferson-Jackson Day dinners. It was she who was in charge of Truman's inaugural ball.

The Broadway musical and later the movie *Call Me Madam* was a fictionalized account of her successful term as Envoy Extraordinary to Luxembourg from 1949 to 1953. She has been a household name ever since.

Alice Longworth Roosevelt has called her "commonplace," but Perle's lack of pretensions and the relaxed atmosphere of her parties are what made her and them so successful. Not only could she produce those in power at "Les Ormes," her Washington mansion, but Perle could prevail upon President Truman to play the piano and Eisenhower to sing.

She was a valued fund-raiser within both parties. She was equally astute with her own money and her fortune is known to be well over $10 million.

She was so infuriated that her candidate Lyndon B. Johnson was not nominated for the Presidency in 1960 that she bolted back to the G.O.P. During the "New Frontier" she was definitely "out." She never regained her stature due partly to failing health.

For a person whose social life was always so public Perle seems to have made an impressive number of genuine friends. Many of those she showed a good time have dropped in to visit her at the Oklahoma City nursing home where she has been residing.

Pearl Bailey is one of Perle's famous friends who have dropped by to see her in Oklahoma City. *(Wide World Photos)*

Harold Peary played Throckmorton P. Gildersleeve on network radio for eleven years. *(CBS Photo)*

THE GREAT GILDERSLEEVE

Throckmorton P. Gildersleeve began in 1938 as a character on Fibber McGee and Molly's [3] radio show. He became so popular that NBC's Red Network gave him a thirty-minute weekly program of his own which premiered on August 31, 1941.

Hal Peary originated the role and in a sense created it by his distinctive voice and mannerisms. Kraft Foods, the show's owner and sponsor, refused to give or sell him an interest in the title. For eleven seasons he was told "maybe next year." In 1950 he refused to sign another contract and was replaced by Willard Waterman who also played it on TV in 1955.

The timing and phrasing of both actors was superb. But it was Gildy's attitude that was so funny. The Gildersleeve laugh was unique and indisputably part of Hal Peary. Waterman never attempted to imitate it.

Gildy was the Water Commissioner of Summerfield and the bachelor uncle of Marjorie (Marylee Robb) and the pestiferous Leroy (Walter Tetley). Other members of the cast were: the druggist Peavey (the late Richard Legrand), whose reply to almost everything was "Well, now, I wouldn't say that"; Floyd the barber (Arthur Q. Brian); Craig Bullard (Tommy Bernard); the irascible Judge Hooker (the late Earle Rosse).

Peary had quite a good singing voice which was put to good use frequently when he sang with the members of his lodge, "The Jolly Boys."

A great ladies' man, he beaued the Southern belle Adeline Fairchild (Una Merkel [3]) and the flirtatious widow Leila Ransom (Shirley Mitchell).

The most popular next to the show's star was Gildy's housekeeper Birdie (the late Lillian Randolph).

Waterman has remained active in all media and had a long run in the Broadway production and the road company of *Mame*. He also played with Rosalind Russell in the movie version of *Auntie Mame* (1958).

Peary is the TV and radio spokesman for Gibraltar Savings and Loan Association of Los Angeles and the honorary mayor of Manhattan Beach. He is also one of that town's largest landowners. He is of Portuguese descent. His wife is Jewish and an electronics engineer. Peary and Waterman have known each other since the mid-thirties and have remained friends to this day.

One season after Gildy began, his Blue Network competition, Mrs. Eleanor Roosevelt, was cancelled. Years later when she met Peary the First Lady greeted him with: "Oh, yes. I believe you're the man the President listened to when I was on the air."

Today Peary is the media spokesman for Gibraltar Savings and Loan in Los Angeles. *(Gene Lester)*

Willard Waterman, who took over the role from Peary, is still acting in New York City.

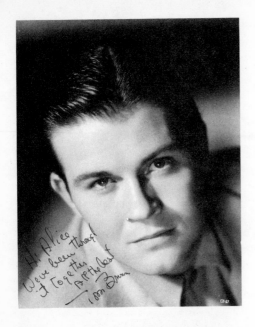

In 1934 Tom was under contract to Universal Pictures. *(Ray Jones)*

TOM BROWN

The all-American boy of 1930s' movies was born Thomas Edward Brown on New York's Lower East Side on January 6, 1913. His mother was Marie Francis, a name in musical comedy, and his father was the late Harry Brown, who was part of the vaudeville team Boyle and Brown. He later made a career of playing drunks in movies.

Tom debuted in vaudeville when he was eighteen months old. At five years he began doing extra work in silent movies. By 1924 he had a feature role in *The Hoosier Schoolmaster* and later *The Lady Lies* (1929).

He did modeling for $2.00 an hour, usually paired with the late Anita Louise. The two attended Professional Children's School along with Helen Mack (who lives in the next apartment to Lanny Ross [1] in Manhattan). Later the mothers of the three founded the still-functioning organization Motion Picture Mothers.

On Broadway Tom did *Is Zat So?* (1925), *Neighbors* (1926), and *Many a Slip* (1930). After the latter folded he came to Hollywood in December of 1931 and was given a test which was written by John Huston. Brown stayed with Universal for three years, long enough to be typecast in the role of kid brother, military cadet, or athlete. Many buffs swear every one of his many features had Brown uttering the same line: "Me now, coach?".

He was *Tom Brown of Culver* (1932), by coincidence playing a part bearing his own name, and then acted in *Anne of Green Gables* (1934), *I'd Give My Life* (1936), and *In Old Chicago* (1938). His favorite role came to him when Mickey Rooney became unavailable for *Navy Blue and Gold* (1937). By the time he entered the army at the outbreak of World War II he was free-lancing and making about $125,000 a year.

Brown was a paratrooper who saw action at the Normandy invasion and went back in service for another two years during the Korean War. He mustered out as lieutenant colonel.

Tom tried playing heavies when he resumed his career but with limited success. Some of his later efforts are: *The Pay-Off* (1942) with Evelyn Brent,[3] *The House on 92nd Street* (1945), *Buck Privates Come Home* (1947), and *Ringside* (1949). In 1952 he toured in *Strike a Match*. Later he attempted to open a theatre-restaurant in San Francisco. Then he conducted hunting tours in the Pacific Northwest. He spent eight years educating himself on the metal magnetite and has developed a mine and built a hotel development in Tahoe Donner, California, where he intends to retire soon.

Tom has finally managed to shake the image of the clean-cut kid. In fact after playing Al Weeks on ABC-TV's *General Hospital* for the past three years he finds that most of the people who recognize him don't even know he had been a movie star thirty years before. The program is seen by twenty million viewers five days a week. But not all have forgotten. Brown, now a grandfather, was seated at a bar when a total stranger walked over and informed him that his wife had always been in love with Tom Brown. Smilingly Tom admitted he was the former star and was then knocked flat on the floor by a punch in the face.

Tom today in his Hollywood apartment next to a caricature of him from the mid-thirties. *(Scott Dean Davis)*

Burt Ward as Robin, the Boy Wonder.

BURT WARD

The Boy Wonder of TV's *Batman* series was born Bert John Gervais, Jr., on July 6, 1945, in Los Angeles. His father owned the *Rhapsody on Ice* show. At Beverly Hills High and during his three years of college Burt maintained an A average. He claims to have been in the top 3 percent of the country in mathematics and science. His I.Q. he says is 147.

When he left UCLA he spent a year attempting to sell real estate. After twelve months he made his first sale to producer Saul David who sent Burt to an agent. The producers of the *Batman* series were looking for a young actor with no experience to play Robin. Ward auditioned and was signed. His salary however was only Screen Actors Guild minimum, although for the second season he was raised $100 a week. The third and final year he received another boost of $50.

Many felt the show's high camp style was actually aided by Burt's lack of professional polish. It was Ward however who accused the crew of being less than competent after he was hospitalized for the fifth time when their fake explosives proved too real. Today he explains his bad press and difficulties with the producers on the fact that he is extremely frank.

One influential Roman Catholic organization was outraged by the fit of Robin's tights. When he donned an athletic supporter they still were not pleased. Even after the network made him wear a second supporter the group complained that his costume was too revealing. "Then," says Ward, "someone at ABC got some kind of a pill I was supposed to take which of course I didn't. I think the next step they were planning was castration."

When the program left the network in 1968 it was among the top ten in ratings. It is still in reruns in the United States and is currently playing around the world, including all of the Iron Curtain countries.

Burt has a daughter by his first wife. He was then married briefly to Kathy Kersh who is now married to Vince Edwards.

The demise of the series catapulted Ward from stardom to almost instant oblivion. He can still command a sizeable fee but the only work he has been able to get is personal appearances at college "camp" festivals and openings of supermarkets. He used to receive 15,000 fan letters a week. Now he averages about 650.

Burt has real Boy Wonder enthusiasm about his future. His apartment overlooking the Pacific Ocean is filled with books on the occult, and Burt believes he is a medium with healing powers. He wants to do "Terry and the Pirates" on TV with his own unit, Puff Productions, and himself in the title role. He is also marketing a felt-tip pen called "Lollipens." At present he spends his time in Malibu with a former Miss France and her mother, and his Siberian husky.

Burt has an apartment right on the Pacific Ocean in Malibu, California. (Michael Knowles)

Of all her serials *The Tiger Woman* (1944) was by far Linda's most successful.

LINDA STIRLING

The serial queen was born Louise Schultz on October 11, 1921, in Long Beach, California. She paid her way through acting school by modeling.

Linda's original goal was the stage but just as she was about to try her luck in New York a role in *The Powers Girl* (1942) came along. Shortly afterward Linda auditioned for Republic Pictures. They asked her if she could ride. She couldn't, but naively felt she could fake it or learn before she had to mount a horse. Although the interview-screen test was a mixture of comedy and near tragedy she did get the contract. The studio intended to use her in their series of serials. Linda felt it would be a stepping stone to more prestigious parts. It wasn't.

Her first, *The Tiger Woman* (1944), with the late Allan "Rocky" Lane was very popular and her fate was sealed. She played the title role in *Zorro's Black Whip* (1944). Then there were *Manhunt of Mystery Island* (1945), *The Purple Monster Strikes* (1945), and *The Crimson Ghost* (1946). Adult moviegoers could have been unaware of her eixstence but Linda Stirling's name meant thrills and excitement to kids who attended the Saturday matinees throughout North America.

She made feaures too but they were limited by her studio's production facilities which were very limited indeed. Some of them were: *San Antonio Kid* (1944), *Santa Fe Saddlemates* (1945) with Sunset Carson (living in Middletown, Kentucky), *The Invisible Informer* (1946), and, her last,

The Pretender (1947). Her personal favorite is *The Madonna's Secret* (1946).

For a girl who has never been athletic and who to this day hates exercise Linda was really put through her paces between serials and westerns. Both required very hard work and subjected her to real danger. Perhaps the most painful part of it all was that kids would cry out "Hey, there's the Tiger Woman!" whenever she appeared in a movie. Major studios simply couldn't take her seriously after she had had so much exposure in serials and cheap westerns.

It took TV to give Linda a chance to act. During the early fifties she appeared on *The Millionaire; Have Gun, Will Travel;* and *Medic,* but by then she was the mother of two boys and had to a great extent lost interest in her career. Linda married Sloan Nibley, writer of many of the Republic epics in 1946.

As her boys entered junior high school Linda entered college. In 1963 she received her B.A. from UCLA and got her M.A. the following year. She commutes daily from her home in North Hollywood to Glendale City College where she teaches English and drama. Asked if her students know about her background she replied: "Every year I wait until one finds out and it's not long before they all know that it's the Tiger Woman up there telling them about Shakespeare."

Linda teaches English and Drama at Glendale College. *(Martitia Palmer)*

The photo that the Soviets wired all over the world to prove they had captured an American agent on May Day, 1960. *(U.P.I.)*

FRANCIS GARY POWERS

The pilot of the history-making U-2 spy plane was a civilian employee of the C.I.A. Before signing on at $2,500 a month for espionage flights, Powers had been a first lieutenant in the U.S. Air Force.

He was born on August 17, 1929. His home town is Pound, Virginia.

Gary had been making flights over the U.S.S.R. since 1956. They were all highly secretive and illegal. His last was made in 1960 from Peshawar, Pakistan, with a destination of Bodö, Norway. Thirteen hundred miles into Russia his plane went down and he parachuted. His superiors had provided him with a poisoned needle in case he wished to commit suicide but he allowed himself instead to be taken prisoner.

At first the Soviets announced only that the U-2 plane had crashed. The United States, thinking that Powers had been killed, promptly denied that he was on an espionage mission. Within hours the Russians called the C.I.A. liars and proved it with a detailed confession from Powers. Moscow had a propaganda field day. The irony of it was that he was captured on May Day, the most honored holiday in the Marxist world.

It was the first time Americans were forced to believe not only that their government was engaged in operations that violated international law but that public officials were capable of lying about anything so serious.

In an angry face-to-face exchange with President Eisenhower Premier Khrushchev cancelled the Paris Summit meeting. The invitation of the American head of state to the Soviet Union, the first in history, was unceremoniously withdrawn.

Powers pleaded guilty and made a public apology. His sentence of ten years' imprisonment was relatively light. Under Soviet law he could have been put to death.

At 8:30 A.M. on February 10, 1962, he was freed. In history's first spy exchange Gary was traded for the top Russian agent Rudolph Abel.

Powers received $52,000 in back salary and continued for a while in the employ of the C.I.A. He then was employed as a test pilot at Lockheed.

Within a year after his release Gary and his wife had divorced and he had remarried. He and his second wife live with their two children in the San Fernando Valley. She is a former psychometrist for the C.I.A.

The former spy is still in the sky. Los Angelenos hear his voice daily on radio station KGIL's "Sky Watch." Powers reports traffic conditions from a helicopter.

Gary Powers. *(Los Angeles Times)*

By the late 1930s Joslyn was a familiar face to moviegoers throughout the world.

ALLYN JOSLYN

The character actor-comedian was born on July 21, 1901, in Milford, Pennsylvania, and brought up in New York City. His father was a mining engineer who lived in Dutch Guiana much of the time. Allyn's mother, who was a nurse, took him to all the Broadway plays and encouraged his interest in acting. He left prep school at sixteen and took a job as an office boy, but after six months of boredom he left to go on the stage.

Margaret Mayo, author of *Twin Beds,* gave him letters of introduction to 23 Broadway producers. The last of the list gave him a small part in *Toot Toot* (1918). Allyn worked a great deal through the twenties but somehow never hit it big until *Boy Meets Girl* (1936) put his name in lights. It was his 36th play. Before that he carried a spear in John Barrymore's *Richard III* (1920), appeared in *The Firebrand* (1924), and had the lead in George M. Cohan's flop *Vermont* (1929). He supported himself during the lean Depression years by working as an assistant stage manager and radio actor. In one play he had only one line consisting of two words. In one period of eighteen months he was in six flops in a row.

Director Mervyn Le Roy saw him in *Boy Meets Girl* and signed him to a two-picture contract. His debut was also Lana Turner's first, *They Won't Forget* (1937). His others include: *Sweethearts* (1938), *Only Angels Have Wings* (1939), *No Time for Comedy* (1940), *The Immortal Sergeant* (1943), and *Junior Miss* (1945).

Joslyn returned to Broadway several times, most notably for the smash hit *Arsenic and Old Lace* (1941). Although he wasn't given the movie

128

version of it or *Boy Meets Girl* it was no great disappointment to him. He took his acting seriously, and Hollywood was and is still something of a joke to him.

Although he was not temperamental neither was he overly impressed with money and power. He turned down a $40,000 offer from Ernest Lubitsch because he didn't like the role and risked suspension at Twentieth Century-Fox when he refused a part in which he was to rape Peggy Ann Garner.[3] Two of his favorite pictures are *Café Society* (1939) in which he was a nance and *Titanic* (1953) where he played a coward who got into drag to save his own skin.

Allyn has worked less and less over the last twenty years. He appeared now and then on the TV series *The Adams Family* in the sixties but his appearances were usually as favors for someone. He doesn't miss acting and isn't a bit tempted by the scripts which are still sent to him.

He and the former stage actress Dorothy Yockel, who has been his wife for over forty years, live in a beautiful house in Beverly Hills. Their one daughter is a psychologist.

Although Joslyn sees almost no one from his years in the studios he loves telling stories about those days. The brunt of the jokes always falls on the monumental egos of the stars, producers, and directors he worked with.

He spends most of his time these days reading but insists his choice in books runs from "junk to trash."

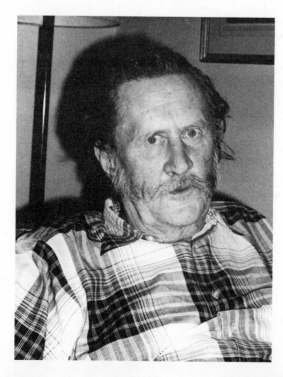

Allyn considers himself completely retired. *(Malcolm Leo)*

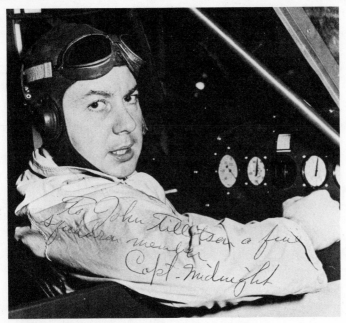

Ed Prentiss posed for this *Captain Midnight* publicity still in 1942.
(John Tillotson Collection)

CAPTAIN MIDNIGHT

It may have been late afternoon by the clock on the mantel but when boys and girls heard the sound of a plane's engine and the toll of a bell striking twelve they were transported to Midnight—the hour when radio's most famous pilot came to the rescue. Monday through Friday the Mutual Broadcasting System presented the fictional hero.

Emanating from WGN in Chicago, *Captain Midnight* was first brought to his listeners by Skelly Oil when he began in 1940 but after the first season Ovaltine dropped their sponsorship of *Little Orphan Annie* in favor of the adult, masculine character.

The Captain was as popular for his offers as for his exploits. It took the inner seal from a jar of Ovaltine to get a *Captain Midnight* "Code-O-Graph" without which a listener was unable to decipher the "secret message" he gave at the end of each fifteen-minute episode. He also gave away an assortment of rings and winged badges (one with litmus paper that changed colors). For 15 cents plus the Ovaltine seal one could obtain an official "Shake-up Mug."

The program was developed by Robert Burtt and Wilfred Moore, both of whom had been aviators in World War I. According to the story Captain Midnight, whose real name was supposed to be Red Albright, had gotten his nickname from his nighttime heroism. His adversary during his lifetime on radio was the international criminal Ivan Shark, played by Boris Aplon (living in New York). Then there was the equally dangerous daughter Fury Shark who was played by both Rene Rodier and Sharon Grainger.

The title role was originated by Ed Prentiss who left it the second season and was replaced by Bill Bouchey. The third year Prentiss was back. He stayed with the part until at the end of the 1948–49 season when he asked for a $25 a week raise. The agency man who turned him down without consulting the sponsor was promptly fired but by then Prentiss had gone to New York to announce for the *Dave Garroway Show*. Paul Barnes played Captain Midnight for the final season.

The hero's young friends were Chuck Ramsey who was usually played by Jack Bibens (living in Chicago) and Joyce Ryan who was Mary Lou Neumayer and Angeline Orr. Their trusted but highly eccentric mechanic was Ichabod Mudd played by Hugh Studeback (living in Los Angeles). Ivan Shark had Gardo, played by Art Hern and Earl George, who helped him menace the good guys.

Kids were not the only ones to take the program seriously. In the fall of 1941 the plot concerned an unnamed foreign power who was attempting to sink a ship in order to block Pearl Harbor in preparation for an air attack. Weeks later the Japanese bombed Pearl Harbor and the F.B.I. visited the producers for a long and grueling interrogation about the striking coincidence.

Ed Prentiss has remained active in radio and TV, playing the part of the banker on the *Bonanza* series and parts in movies such as *The F.B.I. Story* (1959). He lives in Pacific Palisades across the street from Walter Matthau.

In the early fifties Richard Webb played Captain Midnight on television but the series was soon cancelled. Such exciting adventures as the Captain had were not believable on TV. But for a full decade on radio the dashing hero of the skies provided the most exciting excuse a boy or girl ever had for postponing homework.

Ed Prentiss is still an actor and now lives in Pacific Palisades, California. *(Dr. Bill Erwin)*

By 1929 the Foy act consisted of (left to right): Charlie, Mary, Richard, Madeline, Irving, and Eddie, Jr.

THE SEVEN LITTLE FOYS

The Royal Family of Vaudeville was born to Eddie Foy, an enormously popular children's entertainer, and his Italian-born wife, a dancer. In chronological order there were: Bryan, Charlie, Dick, Mary, Madeline, Eddie, Jr., and Irving.

Their family home in New Rochelle, called Foyer, was a haven for theatrical people. When the pastor of the local Roman Catholic church solicited the Foys for a donation he was promised instead a benefit starring some of the biggest names in show business. Eddie, Sr., produced and staged the gala but hours before curtain he got a call from several of the stars. By mistake they had taken the train to Rochelle, New York, and couldn't make the performance. All of the Foy children performed constantly around the house and they were put on stage to fill the gap in the bill. They sang, danced, did imitations of famous personalities of the day and parodies of popular vaudeville turns. All seven were filled with youth, confidence, and talent.

In the audience was E. F. Albee, the adoptive father of playwright Edward Albee. The Foys were promptly booked into Albee's Keith-Orpheum theatre chain. From 1914 until the mid-twenties they toured the nation. It was a fast-paced, sassy act that commanded top billing everywhere.

Bryan co-authored the hit song "Mr. Gallagher and Mr. Sheen." He left the group in 1923 to produce movies. He was for many years the head of B production for Warner Brothers. His most famous films were *Lights of New York* (1928), which was the first all-talking picture, and *House of Wax* (1953), the 3-D thriller.

By the time their dad died in 1928 the Foys were scattered. Charlie had gone out as a single doing impersonations. "I bombed," he says. Five of the Foys reunited in 1929 and were making $1,500 a week when Ziegfeld lured Eddie, Jr., away for $1,000 to play on Broadway in *Show Girl*. He worked steadily in movies, playing his father in both *Frontier Marshal* (1939) and *Lillian Russell* (1940).

From 1941 to 1956 the family occasionally performed together at Charlie Foy's Supper Club in the San Fernando Valley. Charlie is retired now and goes to the race track every single day.

The Foys are still a very close-knit family and see each other constantly. Dick managed a chain of movie theatres until he died in 1947. The only one of the others not living in the Los Angeles area is Irving, who has settled in Albuquerque, New Mexico.

The technicolor musical *The Seven Little Foys* (1955) was made by Paramount starring Bob Hope, a close friend of the Foys. It dramatized the famous Iroquois Theatre fire of December 30, 1903, when 575 people were killed during a performance of *Mr. Bluebeard* starring Eddie, Sr. The tragedy, which occurred in Chicago, changed the fire laws throughout the country. The Foys sold the rights to their careers for a flat fee of $100,000. They had been offered instead a 10 percent cut of the profits. It was a major miscalculation because the picture made millions.

Charlie, Bryan, Mary, Madeline, and Eddie, Jr., pose beneath a picture of their famous father. *(Lauren Eason)*

By the end of World War II "Pappy" had personally brought down 26 Japanese planes. *(Courtesy of United States Marine Corps)*

"PAPPY" BOYINGTON

The flying ace of World War II was born on December 4, 1912, in Coeur d'Alene, Idaho, and brought up in Okanogan, Washington. He was the star of the wrestling team at the University of Washington where he studied aeronautical engineering.

In 1937 Boyington resigned his commission of first lieutenant in the Marine Corps to become a Flying Tiger under the late General Claire Chennault.

He became a Marine again after Pearl Harbor. The first job offered to him was at a desk, which he refused. Although his age and maverick reputation were against him he finally was assigned to lead a group no one else wanted. They were well-trained pilots but had no team spirit. Within the Corps they were referred to as "Boyington's Bastards." The newspapers called them "Black Sheep." Their insignia was a shield outlined in black with a bar sinister running from upper right to lower left denoting illegitimacy. On the shield was a blue Corsair fighter plane and a flop-eared black sheep. In their first action they bagged 11 enemy planes. Within six weeks their kill stood at 58 certain and 22 probable Japanese aircraft. Boyington, whose first name is Gregory, was called "Pappy" because he was the oldest man in the squadron.

In September of 1943 he shot down 5 Zeros in one encounter. On Christmas Eve of that year he took 4 more over Rabaul. In 1944, on the day he shot down his 26th plane, he was captured by the Japanese. When he was released after spending twenty months in a prison camp he received the Congressional Medal of Honor.

His superiors made a great show of his record for a public eager for heroes, but he was a constant irritant to them. While still married he pursued a woman from Bombay to New York and informed her husband that he intended to marry her. Instead he sued her over some money he said he had given her. "Pappy" lost the court case.

After he was mustered out of the service as a full colonel he worked for several aircraft companies but kept in the news with his outspoken remarks. In 1958 his autobiography *Baa, Baa Black Sheep* was a best seller.

"Pappy" has slowed down considerably in the past years due mainly to poor health. He lives alone in Clovis, California, and spends most of his time on his oil paintings. He is not however lacking in frank opinions. On Richard M. Nixon for whom he campaigned several times: "He has the intelligence and courage to be a really great president but he can't be straight with anyone. It just isn't in him." Of the Flying Tigers: "I joined them because I was deeply in debt and they paid very well. I didn't care any more about China than Chennault did. He stole that country blind."

The man who is credited with killing at least 28 Japanese pilots admitted recently that when he was a boy a Japanese had saved his life. "I've always had good relations with them," he said. "They think of us as suckers, which of course we are."

Pappy makes his home now in Clovis, California. (*Alicia Rosinek*)

In 1945 Lee was under contract to Warner Brothers studios.

LEE PATRICK

The popular character actress was born Lee Salome Patrick in New York City on November 22. Her father, the editor of a trade paper, encouraged her interest in the theatre. She took the advice of his friend George Arliss and spent several years getting invaluable training in stock.

Lee debuted on Broadway in *The Green Beetle* (1924). The following year she was in seven flops in a row. It wasn't until 1929 that she landed her first really good part in *June Moon*. She and the play were such hits it was revived with her in it in 1933.

She came to Hollywood for the early talkie *Strange Cargo* (1929) and then returned to the stage for another hit, *Blessed Event* (1932). Her notices from *Stage Door* (1936) brought her offers from four studios. Lee chose RKO so she could repeat her performance in the film version which that studio owned. Instead she was given six B pictures in a row and then saw her *Stage Door* role rewritten for two other actresses, Ginger Rogers and Katherine Hepburn. She moved to Warner Brothers but after a year was dropped in favor of Eve Arden.

With all her stage experience, versatility, and professionalism in her favor Lee also had several things working against her. It simply was not her nature to play studio politics. Also her husband Tom Wood had written quite a frank piece on Louella Parsons in a national magazine in 1939. The late columnist used her considerable influence in both their careers. The only thing Lee could ever put her finger on was the catty remarks Parsons passed from time to time on her radio show and in her column. Another thing against her was her lack of driving ambition. She admits she never yearned to be a star and always put her marriage first.

She always thought of pictures as being a poor second to the stage. She never enjoyed making films and got much more pleasure out of the running part she did for years on the radio series *The O'Neils*.

Her two important near-misses were when Samuel Goldwyn seriously considered her for the title role in *Stella Dallas*. The second was when her agent Zeppo Marx[4] advised her against testing for the part of the prostitute in *Dead End*. It went to Claire Trevor who was nominated for an Academy Award.

Among her 63 features were: *The Sisters* (1938), *Money and the Woman* (1940) with Brenda Marshall (living in Palm Springs, California), *The Maltese Falcon* (1941), *Now, Voyager* (1942), *Mrs. Parkington* (1944), *Mildred Pierce* (1945), *The Snake Pit* (1948), *There's No Business Like Show Business* (1954), *Summer and Smoke* (1961), and *The New Interns* (1964).

By free-lancing Lee avoided being typecast and was able to play dowager, the other woman, lunatic, stripper, and con artist.

Her real claims to fame are the 78 thirty-minute *Topper* TV shows she did from 1953 to 1955, in which she played Mrs. Topper. They are still in syndication and she is recognized more for them than anything else she has done.

Lee and her husband have no children. They live in a home in Westwood, California, filled with the canvases she paints and the cats she spoils. The Woods travel to London every year for a tour of the plays. When a fan complimented her recently on the fine acting jobs she did Lee replied: "Dear, if you like what you saw in those movies you'd be ecstatic over what I did that was cut out!" Lee Patrick has one of the most infectious and most frequently used laughs in Hollywood.

Lee lives with her writer husband in Westwood, California. (*Jerry Mastroli*)

Lois left Paramount Pictures in 1927 after almost a decade under contract.

LOIS WILSON

The star of silent and early talking pictures was born in Pittsburgh on June 28, 1895, and raised in Birmingham. In 1915 she was chosen as the first Miss Alabama in a contest to publicize the newly opened Universal City. The winner of the competition suggested Lois for a part in *The Dumb Girl of Portici* (1916), Anna Pavlova's only feature film. After that she made some J. Walter Kerrigan pictures and then worked with Wallace Reid (his widow, the producer-scenarist Dorothy Davenport Reid, lives a few blocks away from Universal Studios).

Lois was one of the Wampas Baby Stars in 1922, the first year they were picked. Her silents include: *What Every Woman Knows* (1921), *Manslaughter* (1922), *Vanishing American* (1925), *The Gingham Girl* (1927) with George K. Arthur (living on Manhattan's Sutton Place). She was with her friend Valentino in *Alimony* (1924) before he was well known and again in *Monsieur Beaucaire* (1924) at the height of his fame. Her greatest film was the silent classic *The Covered Wagon* (1923).

For years Paramount carefully cultivated her image of the soft, marrying kind of young woman. When Lois fought for and won the part of Daisy in *The Great Gatsby* (1926) her boss Adolph Zukor was furious. *Photoplay* magazine however gave her their Best Performance Award that year and audiences and critics loved her in it.

Her voice, which contains a faint drawl, was perfect for talkies and she made a graceful transition to more mature parts in *Seed* (1931) with the late Helen Parrish. Some of her others of the era were: *Female* (1923) with

Phillip Reed (living in Los Angeles), *The Crash* (1932) with the late Paul Cavanaugh, *Bright Eyes* (1934), *The Return of Jimmy Valentine* (1936) with Charlotte Henry (now the secretary to the Roman Catholic Bishop of San Diego), and *For Beauty's Sake* (1941) with Marjorie Weaver (owner of a liquor store in Brentwood, California). Her last movie was *The Girl from Jones Beach* (1949).

Lois Wilson has been on Broadway a number of times such as in *Farewell Summer* (1937), *Chicken Every Sunday* (1944), and *I Never Sang for My Father* (1968). In the late thirties she toured for 57 weeks in *The Women*.

At her height Lois was an active member of the Hollywood social set. It was in her baby blue Chandler-Six that John Gilbert met Leatrice Joy. She is still in touch with Miss Joy as well as Gloria Swanson, Dickie Moore,[3] Eddie Nugent (San Antonio, Texas) and May Allison (living in Cleveland).

The big love of her life was Richard Dix but she never married him or anyone else.

Miss Wilson sums herself up thusly: "I don't like hippies or long hair or nudity. I guess you could call me a square."

In 1937 Lois moved to New York. She visits her family and friends in Hollywood every year but confessed recently: "I could never live out there again. In Hollywood you're only as good as your last picture. In my town you're as welcome as your greatest success."

Lois owns a garden apartment across from the United Nations Building in Manhattan. *(Michael Harkavy)*

In 1935 Cecilia was put under contract to Metro-Goldwyn-Mayer.

CECILIA PARKER

Andy Hardy's sister, as she was known from her part in twelve of the famous series, was born in Fort William, Ontario, Canada, on April 26, 1914. She was brought up in Hollywood where as a teenager she began working as an extra and doing bit parts in movies such as *The King of Jazz* (1930).

She and her sister Linda played Siamese twins in the talkie version of the Lon Chaney starrer *The Unholy Three* (1930) and repeated their act in Grace Moores's *A Lady's Morals* (1930).

Cecilia got a Fox contract in 1931 and made 20 westerns and 2 serials in one year, after which she was dropped.

She liked making westerns such as *The Rainbow Trail* (1932) with George O'Brien[4] but found the late Ken Maynard[4] "quite impossible."

In 1934 she made *Here Is My Heart* with Bing Crosby, *The Lost Jungle* with the late Clyde Beatty, and then signed an M-G-M stock contract. There was an attempt to create a screen love team of Cecilia with Eric Linden (the father of three, living in Laguna Beach, California, where he inspects roads for the county) and they were paired in several features such as *Ah, Wilderness* (1935) and *Sweetheart of the Navy* (1937). But once she made the first of the highly successful Hardy series, *A Family Affair* (1937), with Julie Haydon (teaching at the College of St. Teresa in Winona, Minnesota) her professional fate was sealed. She did other roles such as Garbo's sister in *The Painted Veil* (1934) but in the public's mind she was "Marian Hardy," daughter of Judge Hardy and sister of Mickey Rooney.

She even tested for Melanie in *Gone With the Wind* but no plum roles came her way. Directors and producers thought that she was simply too closely identified with the part not to be distracting in important roles. She knows for a fact that she lost a Harold Lloyd feature because of that reasoning.

In 1945 Mickey Rooney was drafted, the series ended, and Cecilia retired. In 1937 she had married Dick Baldwin who costarred with her in *Gambling Daughters* (1941). The two have been wheeling and dealing in real estate ever since.

For the past fifteen years the Baldwins have been living in Ventura, California, where they built and until recently ran a large motel. They have two boys and a girl.

Her only return to her profession was when Mickey Rooney talked her into making *Andy Hardy Comes Home* (1958) which was a complete disappointment. In spite of the effect it had on her career Cecilia liked doing the Hardy series but admitted in a recent interview that the sequel was a mistake. "The experience only proved to me what I've heard all my life," said Cecilia. "But I had to learn it for myself—you just can't go home again."

Cecilia and her husband are in real estate in Ventura, California. *(J. Nicolesco-Dorobantzou)*

Tony's largest purse was $54,000 when he tried unsuccessfully to take away Joe Louis's crown on June 28, 1939.

TONY GALENTO

"Two-Ton" Tony was born in Orange, New Jersey, on March 12, 1910. At the age of ten he shined shoes. Later he worked on an ice wagon and as a bouncer. Still he found time to fight with every boy in the neighborhood.

By 1931 he was considered a comer. On the night of August 6 in Detroit he KO'd three men in a row, two in the first round and the third in the third round. In Pittsburgh he knocked out a man in the first four seconds of round one—a record.

It wasn't long before his diet, which included between ten to fifteen bottles of beer a day, moved him from the Middleweight to Heavyweight class. He admits to having been actually drunk in the ring for several of his important bouts.

When he was matched with Joe Louis on June 28, 1939, Tony had by then a record of 51 knock-outs. The bout was in Yankee Stadium and as 34,852 fans watched Tony hurt the World Champion with a blow in the second round and had the Brown Bomber on the canvas in the third.

But Louis who was an 8-to-1 favorite retained his title by knocking Galento out in the fourth.

Less than three months later Tony flattened Lou Nova (living in Los Angeles) but Max Baer beat him into gory submission in 8 vicious rounds the following July. Then Max's brother Buddy KO'd Tony on April 8, 1941. Galento had seven more fights after that and won all by knock-outs but in 1944 he quit boxing.

Tony was a crowd pleaser both as a boxer and later as a wrestler. Newspaper men loved to quote his ghetto grammar and audiences howled as he wrestled an octopus, boxed a kangaroo, and rode a bucking bronco. His wrestling matches with humans were no less ridiculous, and Tony refuses to discuss that period out of embarrassment. "Listen," he said recently, "me and the other bums, we needed the dough. What can I tell you?"

He showed up in some movies: *On the Waterfront* (1954), *The Best Things in Life Are Free* (1956), and *Wind Across the Everglades* (1958).

Until recently he had his own tavern in Orange where he lives now in a senior citizen apartment complex. He has switched from beer to Scotch because of its low sugar content. Tony is a diabetic.

Stories still abound about "Two-Ton" Tony. It is true that he was booed for refusing to shake hands with an opponent and he did have a well-deserved reputation for being a dirty fighter. But he also had a lot of courage in the ring, could take brutal punishment, and delivered a devastating left hook. If Galento at his prime were fighting today he almost certainly would be the World Heavyweight Champion.

Tony is an after-dinner speaker and fund raiser for the Fraternal Order of Eagles. *(Anselma Dell'Olio)*

In 1946 Lee appeared in *The Walls Came Tumbling Down*.

LEE BOWMAN

The leading man of screen and television was born in Cincinnati on December 28, 1914. He helped support his family by singing over local radio stations while studying law at the University of Cincinnati. By 1934, however, he had become so discouraged by the low salaries being offered newly graduated attorneys that he left school.

Lee studied at the American Academy of Dramatic Arts in New York City until he was cast in *Berkeley Square* (1936) on Broadway. The head of Paramount's talent department saw him and he was placed under contract. He made his screen debut in *I Met Him in Paris* (1937) with Fritz Feld (living in Los Angeles).

After two years with Paramount he went to RKO where he was dropped after two films. He left M-G-M after five years. Bowman had complained to Louis B. Mayer constantly about always being cast as the second lead. Mayer suggested he might be happier elsewhere. He was—at Columbia. Harry Cohn gave him top billing, but in movies that were seldom of top quality. He never reached stardom.

Among Lee's 75 features are: *Having a Wonderful Time* (1938), *Love Affair* (1939), *Third Finger, Left Hand* (1940), *Cover Girl* (1944), *Tonight and Every Night* (1945), and *My Dream Is Yours* (1949). His last feature was *Youngblood Hawke* (1964).

He missed out on *Flamingo Road* when Joan Crawford preferred David Brian as her leading man. And, although his father-in-law, Victor Fleming, was the director, he couldn't land the role of the Dauphin in the Ingrid Bergman version of *Joan of Arc*. He lost a Bette Davis picture when the star thought he photographed too young.

The only difficulty he ever had with the many stars he worked with was while making *Smash Up, The Story of a Woman* (1947). Now he feels that the late Susan Hayward was inexperienced and under great pressure.

Bowman played Ellery Queen on TV from 1952 to 1955. Throughout the 1950s he was a frequent guest star on dramatic shows, and he feels the best work of his career was done on the Robert Montgomery [3] presentation of *The Great Gatsby*.

For over thirty years he has been married to his wife Helene, a writer and radio interviewer. They are the parents of a boy and a girl and live in the Mandeville Canyon in Los Angeles. He has remained friends with Cesar Romero (owner of a low-priced men's clothing store in Los Angeles), John Payne,[3] and Steffi Duna, the widow of his close friend Dennis O'Keefe.

Lee gave up acting after a disastrous experience with Elaine Stritch in an off-Broadway production of *Private Lives* in 1968. He is now a special consultant to the chairman of the board of Bethlehem Steel, coaching corporate executives in public speaking. Previously, he worked for five years for the Republican Campaign Committee. His job was to teach GOP politicians camera technique.

Asked if he missed acting he replied: "Not a bit. The only thing my job lacks now is billing. The rest is all there—famous people, travel, and some egos that would put my contemporaries to shame."

Lee Bowman in the study of his Mandeville Canyon home. *(Coleen Magee)*

Some of Olga's Latin temper was caught in this 1948 publicity still.

OLGA SAN JUAN

The Puerto Rican Pepper Pot was born on March 16, 1927, in the Flatbush section of Brooklyn. Her parents returned to Puerto Rico when she was three years old but came back to the United States in 1933 and settled in Spanish Harlem.

Olga began dancing at a very early age and when she wasn't taking lessons she was usually in the movies. Her mother, who loved everything to do with show business, encouraged her daughter. In 1938 she was one of six little girls who performed the Fandango for President Roosevelt at the White House. A few years later Ray Bolger introduced her to a crowd of celebrities and café society at one of the El Morocco's Sunday night shows. From that she was signed by the Copacabana where she performed with two Cuban boys. She was still a teenager when the Paramount Theatre in New York City billed her act as Olga San Juan and Her Rumba Band. Paramount Pictures put her under contract and did rather well by her, considering she was restricted by a heavy Puerto Rican accent. Two of her classmates at the studio's school, now both deceased, were Gail Russell and Diana Lynn. Blondes were "in" and Olga became one.

She was in *Rainbow Island* (1944), *Out of This World* (1945), and *One Touch of Venus* (1948). One of her shorts, *Bombalera* (1944), won an Oscar nomination.

She fought hard for the role of Amber La Vonne in *Variety Girl* (1947) and stood out among an all-star cast. But when Olga lost *The Story of Dr. Wassell* (1944) she was depressed for weeks afterward.

In her films she was often very fiery. Off-screen she was a great favorite among her contemporaries and even managed to get along with the late Sonja Henie [1] when they made *Countess of Monte Cristo* (1948). She worked hard and kept casts and crews constantly entertained with her attempts at English. When asked once by a reporter how she had felt when she learned she was to dance with Fred Astaire in *Blue Skies* (1946) she replied: "I have great confidence in him."

Alan Jay Lerner heard her sing at a Hollywood party and gave her the lead in his Broadway musical *Paint Your Wagon* (1951). After a year in the hit she left to have her second baby. In 1948 Olga had married actor-director Edmund O'Brien. What little she has done since, some TV shows and the feature *The 3rd Voice* (1960), has been at his insistence.

The O'Briens, who are Roman Catholics, live in West Los Angeles. Their two girls and one boy all are interested in performing. Olga still gets more fan mail than her active husband but is almost never recognized in public. She resents very much being thought of as a has-been. Recently she suffered a stroke which has ruled professional activities out of the question.

Olga San Juan with her son Brendan just before her recent stroke. (*Michael Knowles*)

The luscious Anita was chosen one of the Wampus Baby Stars of 1929.

ANITA PAGE

One of the screen's all-time great beauties was born Anita Pomares of Irish-Spanish parentage on August 4, 1910, in Flushing, New York. Her friend, the late Betty Bronson,[3] got her a small role in *A Kiss for Cinderella* (1925). Then she pestered her mother until it was arranged for her to do a bit part in *Love 'Em and Leave 'Em* (1926). Her father disapproved of her ambition but gave her one year to get it out of her system.

Anita and her mother went to Hollywood and had some exceptionally good portraits made of the honey-blonde with skin like a camellia. It was only a matter of months until Anita had to choose among three offers of contracts. She went with M-G-M because they offered her not only more money but started her off in a lead role opposite the late William Haines[4] in *Telling the World* (1928).

She and Joan Crawford shared billing in *Our Dancing Daughters* (1928) and *Our Modern Maidens* (1929) but it was Anita who won the notices and most of the fan mail. Miss Crawford was not appreciative and to this day Anita refuses to discuss her.

Anita Page's appeal was very visual and in spite of a voice that is less than soothing she retained her popularity in talkies. Charles King sang "You Were Meant for Me" to her in *Broadway Melody* (1929), a song written by Nacio Herb Brown who was her husband briefly in 1934. Some of her other pictures were: *Our Blushing Brides* (1930), *The Easiest Way* (1931), *Night Court* (1932). But after leaving the Culver City lot in 1932 Anita went quickly downhill via poverty row quickies like *Jungle Bride* (1933), *The Phantom Broadcast* (1933), and *Hitch Hike to Heaven* (1936).

Anita played opposite stars like Clark Gable and the late Ramon Novarro.[1] Germany's Prince Louis Ferdinand dated her after his relationship with Lili Damita (Mrs. Allen Loomis of Fort Dodge, Iowa) ended. She was something of an obsession with Benito Mussolini. She got the big rush from Howard Hughes, Billy Rose, and movie mogul Carl Laemmle, Jr. (living in Beverly Hills). Through it all she had a good reputation and her Catholicism was featured in her publicity. Some feel it may also have restricted her career. As one long-time Hollywood observer put it with a wink: "Anita Page could have gone much further if she'd only gone a bit further."

Anita is now a grandmother by her oldest daughter. Her youngest girl is studying acting. Their mother is very outgoing and thoroughly enjoys giving and attending parties. The family have lived in the Philippines, Washington, D.C., and Hawaii.

In one of her movies, *The Flying Fleet* (1929), which was set in Coronado, California, the script had Anita falling madly in love with a young naval officer. In 1937 after a nineteen-day courtship she eloped with a flyer in the U.S. Navy. He is now a retired admiral and they live in Coronado. Asked recently if it all worked out as well as it seems to observers, the former star replied: "I often think to myself, boy, have I been lucky. I don't know anyone who has had a better life than this gal."

Linda House, Ret. Admiral Herschel A. House, and Anita in their home in Coronado, California. *(Michael Knowles)*

Columbia Pictures starred Edith for the first time in *Little Miss Roughneck* (1938).

EDITH FELLOWS

The movie moppet was born in Boston on May 20, 1923. When her mother disappeared when Edith was two years old her grandmother took her to North Carolina. She was so pigeon-toed an osteopath suggested she be given dancing lessons. By 1926 she had developed into a local name entertainer in school plays. An agent saw her and suggested she be brought to Hollywood where he felt he could get her into pictures. When grandmother Fellows and Edith arrived they found the agent's address to be a vacant lot. Her grandmother did housework to support them, taking Edith along. When one matron objected she left her with a neighbor. The neighbor's little boy, who was an actor, got a call from the casting director of Hal Roach studios. His mother was forced to take Edith along on the interview. The boy got the part in *Movie Night* (1929) but then came down with chicken-pox. Edith filled in, making her debut in the Charlie Chase two-reeler. After that she began working regularly as an extra and bit player.

She was in *Cimarron* (1931) and *Daddy Long Legs* (1931) but briefly. She still has fond memories of Richard Dix's kindness during her first real part in his picture *His Greatest Gamble* (1934). She was a stand-out in *She Married Her Boss* (1935) and was signed to a contract by Columbia Pictures.

The guiding force behind Edith's career and personal life was her late grandmother, a fiercely ambitious woman who insisted on perfection from Edith in everything she did. When in 1936 her mother reappeared and demanded her daughter's return, the grandmother fought her successfully in a messy and, for Edith, a painful court fight. One thing she could not be accused of doing was spoiling her granddaughter. Harry Cohn, the studio head, called her to his office once and strongly suggested she get Edith some decent clothes.

Edith specialized in brat and wallflower roles. She developed quite a following from her appearances in *Mrs. Wiggs of the Cabbage Patch* (1934), *Pennies From Heaven* (1936), and a series which began with *Five Little Peppers and How They Grew* (1939). Filmologist Don Miller has written of her: "Of all the precocious tots at the time she was the least affected and certainly the best actress." She also had a very pleasant singing voice.

Her teenage pictures were *Her First Romance* (1940) with Julie Bishop (Mrs. William Bergin of Beverly Hills) and Alice White (single and living in Hollywood), *Her First Beau* (1941), and *Girl's Town* (1942). Then she replaced Joan Roberts (living in Rockville Center, New York) in *Marinka* (Broadway wags dubbed the musical "Marinka the stinker") (1945). Her greatest professional disappointment was when she lost the lead in the road tour of *Peter Pan* in 1950 because of her height—4 feet 10½ inches. Her last Broadway play was *Uncle Willie* (1956).

Edith has one child, Kathy Fields, an actress, by her first husband Freddie Fields who is head of the talent agency CMA. She was divorced for the second time in 1970.

In 1958 her faltering career and years of repressed anxiety caught up with her in the Orient where she was on tour. She froze in front of an audience and has never performed since. She now lives in Los Angeles and hopes to be able to resume her career soon. In the meantime she supports herself as a switchboard operator.

Edith shares her Los Angeles apartment with several cats. *(Peaches Poland)*

"The Voice Gorgeous" was brought to Hollywood by M-G-M in 1936.

MILIZA KORJUS

The singer who made one movie, was nominated for an Oscar, and then virtually disappeared was born in Warsaw, Poland on August 18. Miliza's voice even at age six was an octave higher than anyone else's and she was noticed almost from the day she began singing in the church choir.

By the time she was eight years old she had developed quite a following from her appearances on Radio Sweden. She was offered a contract but her father who was in the Swedish foreign service moved the family to Finland. Miliza was then taken to Germany and finally Vienna, all the time continuing her vocalizing.

She was in her early teens when she made her debut with the Vienna State Opera in *The Magic Flute* with Richard Strauss conducting.

Miliza sang with the Vienna and Berlin State Operas but it was from her work on radio that she became well known all over Europe.

When M-G-M asked her to play Carla Donna, mistress to Johann Strauss, she brazenly asked the same salary as Greta Garbo. Her demands were met and she arrived in Hollywood in 1936. Metro's brass took one look at her girth and sent her straight to a reducing farm.

Louis B. Mayer could not pronounce either of her names and dubbed her "Gorgeous" which rhymes with Korjus. In her publicity she was referred to as "Miliza Korjus, the Voice Gorgeous."

The Great Waltz was a big hit in 1938 due to a great extent to Miliza. Not only did she have an extraordinary coloratura-soprano but she was indeed gorgeous with one of the most infectious smiles ever photographed. She stole every scene she and her leading man, the late Fernand Gravet, had together. According to Miliza, her costar Luise Rainer[1] who was famous for her crying scenes shed real tears when she read the reviews. It was Korjus's picture and she was nominated for the Academy Award.

Her studio was preparing *Countess Maritza* and *The Merry Widow* for her when she was in a serious auto accident in 1940. After a year in the hospital there was extensive therapy. During her recuperation she regained all the weight she had lost. She made a Mexican film, *Caballeria del Imperio* (1942), and concertized occasionally but her career never regained its momentum.

Madame Korjus still makes recordings for her own label, Venus. She is a widow and lives in a home in Beverly Hills which was built by Mario Lanza. Two of her close friends are the Polish opera singer Ganna Walska (living in Montecito, California) and Kathryn Grayson. She is in the process of turning her home into a museum to be called "The Great Korjus."

Asked if she feels her shortened career was a tragedy she replied in her heavy European accent, "No, because maybe if I make more pictures they would not be so good. And this way I remain very mysterious. You see, I have always wanted to be a legend."

Madame Korjus at a recent motion picture premiere. (M-G-M)

Richard Widmark took over the role of Front Page Farrell in 1941. *(NBC Photo)*

FRONT PAGE FARRELL

The first live network radio serial to originate from New York City began over the Mutual Broadcasting Company on June 23, 1941. It survived for thirteen years.

The situations on the fifteen-minute programs were less outlandish than most of the soap operas of its day. The show's introduction was a simple one: "David Farrell, a crusading New York *Eagle* reporter, and his wife, Sally, often find themselves involved more deeply than they intend to be in some of the stories that David covers for his paper."

Farrell was heard at 5:00 P.M. E.S.T. The producers, Frank and Anne Hummert, reasoned that men who returned home in the late afternoon would enjoy it and that housewives would identify with Sally Farrell and her excitement-filled marriage.

Carleton Young was the first David Farrell and then a relatively unknown young actor named Richard Widmark took over. Staats Cotsworth inherited the part in 1946 and was still playing it when its theme, "You and I Know," was last heard over the airways in 1954. Florence Williams (now Mrs. Andrew Marshall of Mahopac Falls, New York) was Sally.

Cotsworth's other long-running title role on radio was *Casey, Crime Photographer* which he starred in from 1944 to 1955. The late John Gibson played Ethelbert, the bartender of the Blue Note Cafe, a character almost as popular as Casey.

During and after his career on radio Cotsworth appeared in plays on Broadway and in summer stock. Until 1971 he was married to Muriel Kirkland who also had a distinguished career both in the theatre and on radio. In 1932, four years before he met his wife, Staats had dated Josephine Hutchinson when the two were apprentices in Eva Le Gallienne's theatre group. In 1972, a year after he was widowed, Cotsworth called her in Los Angeles after watching her most memorable movie *Oil for the Lamps of China* (1935) on the late show. They were married a few months later.

The Cotsworths live in a Manhattan penthouse filled with Staats's oil paintings which have earned him several awards and a one-man show. He was delighted recently to play a part on the revival of dramatic radio, CBS Radio Mystery Theatre.

Josephine Hutchinson and Staats Cotsworth live in a Manhattan penthouse. *(Richard Schaeffer)*

A 1940 publicity still wishing Sandy's fans a happy Easter.

BABY SANDY

The star who became a has-been when she was four years old was born
Sandra Lea Henville two months prematurely on January 14, 1938, in Los
Angeles.

Her father who was a milkman read in the paper that Universal Pictures
was looking for a ten-month-old baby to play with Bing Crosby in *East
Side of Heaven* (1939). When he left milk that morning on the doorstep
of Charles Previn, the studio's musical director (he was also the father
of André Previn), he included some snaps of Sandy. Previn showed the
pictures to the film's director David Butler who hired her.

Sandy was on the picture two days before someone discovered that she
was a girl. Although the script called for a boy by that time she had
done so well there was no thought of replacing her. Sandy's chief virtue
was that when placed between two adults she would look from one to the
other as they spoke. Graham crackers were used to bribe her for special
scenes such as climbing out on ledges and in front of automobiles. Audiences loved it and Universal signed her to a contract which began at $50
a week. Her mother was paid another $100 to be with her at all times.
She was the first baby star since Baby Le Roy (Leroy Overacker is now a
merchant seaman), and the studio's publicists made the most of it. She
rated two pages in *Life*, and *Look* spread the story of Sandy over four
pages. There was a Baby Sandy mug, a doll, diapers, a pull-toy, the Baby

Sandy story book and a coloring book. All this provided the Henvilles with much more money than their salaries. The little star was represented by the same agent that Deanna Durbin had.

She starred in *Unexpected Father* (1939) with Donald Woods (a real estate agent in Palm Springs, California) and *Little Accident* (1939). She developed such a following that her name became part of the title in *Sandy Is a Lady* (1940) with Fritz Feld (living in Los Angeles) and *Sandy Gets Her Man* (1940).

Today her single recollection of her career is the one line "I'd rather be in kindergarten" which she delivered in her last movie, *Johnny Doughboy* (1942).

Sandy, now Mrs. Magee of Highland Park, California, recently gave her first and only interview in which she said that her parents almost never referred to her career after it ended. Nor does she discuss it now with her husband and her three sons. Her husband is a carpet layer. Sandy is a legal secretary for the County of Los Angeles.

Occasionally she watches herself on the late show but thinks the plots of her films are hopelessly corny and that she was a hammy brat.

"When I was about thirteen," she says, "I was going to take drama lessons and become a big star again but my mother thought that was ridiculous. I suppose she was right. The thought of even being in a play terrified me. It still does."

She has no memory of ever having even met a movie star and has no idea of what the inside of a studio looks like. Most of the money she made is still in the bank.

Baby Sandy is a sec
retary, housewife
and mother today
(Ron Alexander)

David posed in his dad's sport coat for this 1955 publicity still.

DAVID NELSON

Ozzie and Harriet's older son was born in New York City on October 24, 1936.

David was twelve years old when he and his brother Ricky asked to be on their parents' show after their playmate, Bing Crosby's son, had guested. From the outset the experience proved traumatic. The first time he saw the rushes he cried. Ricky got all the laughs, which were often at David's expense. "I never held myself in as high regard after that," he has said. He didn't however complain because, "I always tried never to offend anyone. I felt I had a great responsibility not to let my family down." He says that at the age of thirteen he was "a little old man."

He made features such as *Peyton Place* (1957) and *The Big Circus* (1959) and developed a following almost as large as Ricky's. But during that same period he thought he was overweight and wondered if girls went out with him only because he was famous. He was a perfect example of his age group, who were dubbed at the time the "Silent Generation."

In 1961 he married actress June Blair at the chapel in Forest Lawn Cemetery. She was immediately written into the show as a regular. It made their relationship with each other awkward and so typecast her as David Nelson's wife that her career has never recovered.

Before the series expired in 1966 his father allowed him to direct eleven episodes. The credits did him little good however, since it was felt around Hollywood that the show really directed itself. He has since directed several TV shows and made a documentary of his brother on tour. Although the TV commercial company he formed has barely broken even, he has suffered no hardship. When he turned twenty-one David came into a trust fund of his earnings which amounted then to $250,000.

In the fall of 1973 when his parents returned to television in *Ozzie's Girls*, David was announced as director. He assured interviewers that his dad was a professional and could easily take direction even from his own boy. When the series went on the air David was listed as producer.

He is still close to his brother but spends very little time with his parents away from the studio. Their ideas on almost everything differ greatly.

The Nelsons live with their two sons in Toluka Lake in the San Fernando Valley. He and his wife have both had analysis but feel their real breakthrough came with religion: "Our life really began when we accepted Jesus Christ as our Savior."

David Nelson today.
(Carl Charlson)

The main thing Guy Madison had
going for him was his looks.

GUY MADISON

The heart-throb of the forties and TV western star of the fifties was born
Robert Moseley on January 19, 1922, in Punkin Center, California.

He was stationed at the U. S. Navy Base in San Diego when Henry
Willson, who was in charge of talent for Selznick-International Films,
spotted him in the audience of a radio show. The program featured
Janet Gaynor [2] who was introducing a young singer named Suzanne Bruce.
Willson took them both to Selznick's studio where their names were
changed to Guy Madison and Jane Powell.

David O. Selznick put him in several brief but effective scenes in *Since
You Went Away* (1944). The bobbysoxers squealed and the fan magazines
predicted he would be a big star.

Selznick got Madison discharged from the service six months early in
order to play opposite Dorothy McGuire in *Til the End of Time* (1946).
He was in *Honeymoon* (1947) with Shirley Temple and Lina Romay (living
in Los Angeles).

Shrewdly Selznick publicized his handsome star and then loaned him
to other studios for substantial fees. Guy studied very hard at acting school
but he never became more than adequate.

Some of his features were: *Massacre River* (1949), *The Charge at Feather
River* (1953), *5 Against the House* (1955) with Kerwin Matthews, and
Hilda Crane (1956).

When Selznick dropped him he went to the cheapie studio Monogram. It was the TV series *Wild Bill Hickok* that brought him back. As part owner along with his agent Helen Ainsworth he made a fortune from the 113 thirty-minute episodes filmed between 1951 and 1958. He also starred on the radio show *Wild Bill Hickok,* and received royalties from all the *Hickok* merchandising. Rodeo appearances were also very lucrative.

He spent from 1962 to 1969 in Italy making 31 features such as *Shatterhand* (1967) with the late Lex Barker and *Payment in Blood* (1968) with Edd "Kookie" Byrnes (living in Los Angeles).

Guy was married to the late Gail Russell from 1949 to 1954. After their divorce he married Sheila Connolly. The couple separated in 1960 and were divorced three years later. They have three daughters.

In 1971 Madison announced that he would produce and star in several features but they were never filmed. Much of the money he made was lost in bad investments. In 1973 he toured the Midwest in a play. Guy lives alone in Hollywood. He has remained very close to his children. Even in his heyday he was never very social and still spends a great deal of time hunting and fishing.

Guy is still seen around Hollywood at parties and openings. *(Frank Edwards)*

Karl Swenson as Lorenzo Jones ponders one of his absurd inventions for a 1948 publicity photo. *(National Broadcasting Company)*

"LORENZO JONES"
KARL SWENSON

The impractical, naive, and extremely likeable character was first heard on the NBC Radio Network on August 26, 1937. The fifteen-minute, five-time-a-week show was produced by the prolific team of Frank and Anne Hummert and written by Theodore and Mathilde Ferro (The Ferros are now working on TV's *The Guiding Light*).

Lorenzo worked as a mechanic at Jim Barker's garage but his heart was always with his inventions. It was about those contraptions that many of the plots centered. Most of his ideas were impossible or foolish in concept like his three-spout teapot. One of the last episodes had Lorenzo's boss driving along the highway listening to a recorded voice telling him that he had just passed the speed limit. The voice and the invention were Lorenzo's. Some of the gadgets which the authors felt at the time were absurd turned out to be not only useful but are things Americans today take for granted. To radio listeners in pre-World War II America steam-heated sidewalks may have sounded outlandish but they have been in use for many years in downtown areas. The outdoor vacuum cleaner brought great guffaws when Lorenzo described it but thousands of these machines are used daily in recreational areas.

Lorenzo Jones was aired in the late afternoon and the whimsy of the plots came as balm to the weary ear of anyone who had their radios on all day. The program was not a soap opera in the usual sense in that it had an extremely light touch. Its theme was the upbeat "Funiculi, Funicula" and its announcer Don Lowe always called it "a story with more smiles than tears." And so it was until 1952. Ratings of all the daytime shows were slipping and the Hummerts decided to make *Lorenzo Jones* into a melodrama. Critics, listeners, and cast all disapproved and the series ended in 1957.

In nineteen years Karl Swenson missed playing the title role only once when he was snowbound. The late Alan Bunce filled in for him. He had come to radio from the stage and has continued successfully after *Lorenzo* on TV and in movies. His skills as an actor are such that he could play the loveable small-town dreamer Lorenzo Jones during the same years he was heard daily as Lord Henry Brinthrop, the elegant husband of *Our Gal Sunday*.[4] Recently Swenson referred to that character as "a male chauvinist pig."

He lives in South Laguna, California, with his wife of over twenty years, Joan Tompkins. Ms. Tompkins played Fay, daughter of *Ma Perkins*,[3] and the title roles in *Lora Lawton* and *Nora Drake* on radio.

Lorenzo Jones married Nora Drake and they live in South Laguna, California. *(Dick Lynch)*

In 1924 Viola was in *Merton of the Movies.*

VIOLA DANA

The star of silent pictures was born Viola Flugrath in Brooklyn on June 28, 1897. Her mother had wanted a career of her own and put her daughters on the stage when they were very young. Viola was one of the children in the Broadway play *Rip Van Winkle* (1905) and by 1910 was working steadily without billing in movies being made at Edison's studio in the Bronx.

After playing the title role in the hit play *Poor Little Rich Girl* (1913) she was starred in her films. Her contract was signed with Metro Pictures before it became part of M-G-M. In order to get her they had to hire her husband Johnny Collins, who came along as her director.

While taxes then were minimal agents for stars were almost unheard of. The most Viola ever made was $1,750 a week even when she free-lanced after her seven-year contract had expired.

Some of her pictures were: *The Parisian Tigress* (1919), *Revelation* (1924), and *Kosher Kitty Kelly* (1926).

Her younger sister had also made a name for herself in movies as Shirley Mason. Both were casualties of sound. They appeared together at the end of their careers in the early talkie musical *Show of Shows* (1929). By then Viola's first husband had died.

She took singing lessons from Marion Davies's coach and when there were no calls from the studios she went on a vaudeville tour in the skit *The Ink Well* by Anita Loos. By the time it was clear there would be no offers of parts in talking pictures she was happily married to the golf pro

Jimmy Thompson. They followed the golfing tournaments all over the country until their friendly divorce in 1945.

Viola was so popular as a visiting Blue Lady at the Motion Picture Country House and Hospital that its residents gifted her with a ruby pin.

During a recent interview Viola said of herself and her sister, "We always got what we wanted for as long as I can remember." She was the bigger star but feels that Shirley had more success in her private life. When her husband, the director Sidney Lanfield, died in 1972 they had been married for 45 years.

Both sisters kept their figures, their sense of humor, and enough of the money they made to afford a very comfortable life style. They are still very close.

Shirley lives in an apartment at Marina Del Rey, California, and is a grandmother. Viola lives near the Pacific Ocean in Santa Monica. Her closest friend, TV star Irene Ryan, died in 1973. She still sees Evelyn Brent [3] and Ruth Clifford (living in Beverly Hills). To keep busy she works several days a week at Skillets, a shop in Westwood Village.

Recently Viola summed up the attitudes of her sister and herself toward Hollywood now: "In our day it was considered daring if fan magazines carried a story on us behind the make-up. Today they make up the behinds."

Viola and her sister Shirley Mason are still very close. (John Scott Miller)

Janet Waldo played Corliss Archer on radio until the program went off the air in 1956. (*CBS Photo*)

CORLISS ARCHER

The fictitious teenage girl debuted over the CBS Radio Network as a summer replacement show in 1943. It was taken to ABC, moved to Mutual and wound up on NBC. It was cancelled several times. But *Corliss* survived for thirteen years.

A few weeks after the program began Priscilla Lyon was replaced in the title role by Janet Waldo. David Hughes, who played her boyfriend Dexter, died during the program's first year and Sam Edwards took over. Like Janet he remained on the series until its demise in 1956.

The character of Corliss Archer was inspired by the two daughters of its creator, F. Hugh Herbert. He originally wrote about her in short stories for *Cosmopolitan* magazine. Then in 1943 Joan Caulfield played her in the Broadway hit *Kiss and Tell*.

Although she was supposed to be the typical teenage girl of the time, in retrospect the character seems not very bright and emotionally unstable. Janet Waldo, who says that she identified strongly with Corliss, describes her as "an extrovert." On most of the thirty-minute shows she was hysterical with happiness or a fountain of tears. She was very flirtatious but never wore lipstick. On rare occasions Corliss and Dexter would hold hands "but I'm sure they never kissed," said Janet recently.

The program began each week with: "She's only fifteen but she'll love you forever if you think she's much, much older. Ladies and gentlemen, meet Corliss Archer, starring Janet Waldo." Its star had been discovered and brought to Hollywood in 1939 by Bing Crosby. During the year she was under contract to Paramount she did bit parts and leads in low-budget westerns. Her star billing, a very rare thing in radio, still seems impressive.

Since 1949 Janet has been married to Robert E. Lee, the co-author of such plays as *Inherit the Wind* and *Auntie Mame*. She has never ceased working but most of her roles have been as teenagers such as Emmy Lou on the *Ozzie and Harriet Show*. Even today she specializes in teenage voices on radio and recordings. She is currently heard as the voices of Morticia and Granny on the TV series *The Addams Family*.

Janet still sees Sam Edwards whom she always calls Dexter. She feels young girls today still behave much like the character she played twenty years ago. "My teenage daughter deals with boys just like Corliss or I would," she told an interviewer. When asked if the boys were as willing to be put upon as Dexter she replied, "Of course. Men are long-suffering. They're supposed to be."

Janet Waldo during an interview in her San Fernando Valley home with Richard Lamparski. *(Steve Webster)*

After her reign as Miss America, Jo-Carroll signed a contract with Twentieth Century-Fox studios.

MISS AMERICA OF 1942

"The Texas Tornado," the nickname given to Jo-Carroll Dennison by the press during her reign as Miss America, was born in Florence, Arizona, on December 16, 1923.

Jo-Carroll wasn't a bit drawn to contests. She was working in the office of Senator Earl Mayfield when she won her first, Miss Citizens National Bank, and had to be talked into that. More coaxing got her to compete for the next three but she won them all: Miss Tyler, Texas, Miss East Texas, and Miss Texas.

Not only had she never heard of the Miss America Pageant, but when it was explained and described to her the only thing that made her consent to enter was the chance that she might win a new car even if she didn't take the title. She was not expecting to come in first and the possibility that she might did not appeal to her. Jo-Carroll still had unpleasant memories from childhood of traveling with her parents singing and dancing with a medicine show, and the Miss America Pageant sounded like a repeat. Her goal in life was to raise a family with a handsome husband in a white house on a hill.

She wore a cowgirl outfit and brought the house down singing *Deep in the Heart of Texas.* Then she set some sort of precedent by not crying when she was crowned. For the next twelve months she proved an exceptionally popular Miss America. It was the height of World War II and her figure and heavy drawl went over very well at service installations and bond rallies. She endorsed hats and Catalina swimsuits. One immediate effect of the coronation at the Warner Theatre in Atlantic City was that Jo-Carroll's boyfriend back home wired his congratulations and his regrets that their relationship had just ended.

Jo-Carroll made brief appearances in the films *Winged Victory* (1944) and *The Jolson Story* (1946). A year after making *Diamond Horseshoe* (1945) with Phil Silvers she married him. In 1950 they were divorced.

She became the assistant casting director for Rogers and Hammerstein and then spent time in Israel and Paris for film series that were never produced. In 1954 she married a CBS executive while working as production assistant on the *Lux Video Theatre.*

Today she lives in West Los Angeles with her two teenage sons and her husband whom she refers to as "Prince Charming." They share a white house that overlooks a canyon.

Jo-Carroll outside her hilltop house in West Los Angeles. *(Donna Schaeffer)*

Donna received the Academy Award for the Best Supporting Actress in *From Here to Eternity* in 1953.

DONNA REED

The Oscar winner and TV star was born Donna Belle Mullenger on January 27, 1921, in Denison, Iowa. She grew up on a farm and was the beauty queen of her high school.

Donna enrolled at Los Angeles City College for a business course but her appearances in plays on campus brought her an M-G-M contract. Her rural, Middle-America background was touted by the studio's press department and was followed up by casting her in "girl-next-door" roles.

Her screen test was made with the late Van Heflin who was in her second film *The Get-Away* (1941). For that picture and *Babes in Arms* (1939) before it she was billed as Donna Adams.

Among her credits are: *Mokey* (1942) with the current star Robert Blake playing her stepson, *The Human Comedy* (1943) with Butch Jenkins,[3] *Gentle Annie* (1944) with James Craig (now a real estate dealer in Huntington Beach, California), *The Picture of Dorian Grey* (1945) with Hurd Hatfield (living in Stony Brook, New York), *Faithful in My Fashion* (1946) with Tom Drake,[4] and *Saturday's Hero* (1951) with John Derek.[4]

A new Donna Reed was supposed to emerge from her Academy Award winning performance as the prostitute in *From Here to Eternity* (1953). But the whore she portrayed was at heart a decent girl who longed for "a man of her own." No Hollywood star is more aware of the sexism she was subjected to than Donna Reed. Her "goody-good" parts continued, and on her TV series *The Donna Reed Show* she was the ideal mother and wife. It began September 24, 1958, and made her a millionaire. Today she speaks with contempt of the two-dimensional stereotyped woman she played on it. Her main reason for remaining almost completely retired since it went into syndication in 1966 is her disdain for the male mentalities and egos that control TV programming.

Donna had a brief, early marriage to the make-up man William Tuttle and a second to producer Tony Owen that lasted until 1971.

She was a highly vocal opponent of the U.S. involvement in Vietnam and co-chairperson of "Another Mother for Peace." Her two sons were both conscientious objectors.

The warmth that Donna brought to all those wholesome roles is nowhere evident today when she talks of TV and movies. She feels the image of woman in both is a complete male fantasy. If she ever returns to the screen it most likely will be with a woman as her producer.

Donna on a recent date with Colonel Asmus in Hollywood. *(Frank Edwards)*

Ricky and Desi Arnaz in a 1956 publicity still.

RICKY KEITH

The boy who became nationally famous playing Lucille Ball's son was born Keith Thibodeaux on December 1, 1950, in Lafayette, Louisiana. When his father brought him home from his first parade at ten months he began accompanying music on the radio by playing a knife and fork. For his second Christmas his parents gave him a drum. By 1954 he was the talk of his neighborhood. When Horace Heidt [2] brought his Youth Opportunity show to town, friends insisted Keith be entered in the competition. Keith won the local contest and was such a crowd pleaser he went on tour with Heidt for a year, ending up in Los Angeles.

A friend told his dad that Desilu Studios was looking for a little boy for one of their TV series. Mr. Thibodeaux took his son to the casting department mainly because, like most other Americans, he was an *I Love Lucy* fan and was anxious to see the lot where the series was made.

Aside from his name, which they changed to Ricky Keith, Desi and Lucy liked everything about him. He was a miniature Desi Arnaz in appearance

172

and, like Arnaz, was quite a drummer. He was six years old when he signed with them at a beginning salary of $300 a week. For the next three years he played the son of the most popular couple in America on the nation's highest-rated TV show.

Even after the program went off the network in 1959 Ricky continued acting on shows like *Hazel, Andy Griffith,* and *Route 66.* "But," says Ricky, "I got very tired of this kind of life and wanted normal kid things."

In 1965 the Thibodeaux were divorced and his mother and all the children went back to Lafayette. Ricky returned too and went back to his original name.

After finishing high school he attended college for a year and then became part of a rock and roll group called David and the Giants, playing drums and singing. That lasted for three years and then he returned home and worked for a while on an off-shore oil rig. He is still in Lafayette and hopes to get his own musical group together soon.

Keith says Lucy and Desi always treated him very well although he hasn't heard a word from either in many years.

Ricky has moved back to his home town and assumed his original name.

Stymie made 40 *Our Gang* comedies.

MATTHEW BEARD, JR.

Stymie of *Our Gang* was born in Los Angeles on New Year's Day, 1925. His father was a minister of the Church of God in Christ. Throughout most of his childhood Matthew's parents were separated.

His mother got him a part in *Uncle Tom's Cabin* (1927) when he was only seventeen months old. Then when he was five his father heard Hal Roach Studios needed a replacement for Farina. Matthew flashed a dazzling smile and won the part over 500 others. He appeared in eight two-reelers a year over the next five years.

Although he has not seen any of the other children from the shorts for many years he has fond memories of both the work and the play on the Roach lot. Among his friends were Patsy Kelly,[1] Charlie Chase, Laurel and Hardy. The role he played, however, embarrasses him still. "We knew even then that Stymie was an insult to our race," he allowed recently, "but it was the Depression and I had seven sisters and six brothers at home."

Matt's salary which began in 1930 at $100 a week had been raised to $500 by the time he outgrew the role and was let go in 1935. The life that he had come to love and thought would go on forever had ended and the ten-year-old boy was devastated.

174

He managed to get work in movies from time to time in features such as *Captain Blood* (1935), *Jezebel* (1938), and *Stormy Weather* (1943) but not being under contract he now had to attend public schools. His tutoring on the Roach lot had put him two grades ahead of boys his age and he was promptly demoted. The other children in the ghetto school envied his fame and taunted him constantly. "It wasn't *my* fault I was a star," he says laughingly.

He was using drugs even before graduating from high school. Being Stymie didn't matter a bit in the dives and prisons he spent so many of his adult years in. "I was just another junkie doing time," he says. Even after his release in 1963 after serving part of a twenty-year sentence for heroin he returned to narcotics. But during a thirty-day stretch for petty theft he took a long, hard look at his prospects and went to Synanon, the rehabilitation center in Santa Monica, California.

He now tours grammar schools showing his films and talking to the kids about the thirty-year drug nightmare he lived through.

Matthew has stepchildren and grandchildren by the woman he married in 1968. She is also a Synanon resident and an arrested alcoholic.

In 1973 he met Mario Machado, an interviewer for CBS-TV, who introduced him to an agent. Since then he has been cast in small but good parts in *Hawkins* and *Sanford and Son*. He will be also in the Isaac Hayes feature *Truck Turner*.

Behind the Synanon building which is on the Pacific Ocean is a play-ground full of his new fans who watch the old comedies on TV under the title *Little Rascals*. One little girl recently pointed to the huge structure which houses hundreds of former drug addicts and asked a playmate, "Do you know what that is?" "Yes," replied her friend. "That is the house of Stymie."

Stymie and his granddaughter Diane. *(Michael Knowles)*

Dorothy McGuire is credited with popularizing the natural look among young women in the 1940s.

DOROTHY McGUIRE

The genteel star of stage and movies was born on June 14, 1918, in Omaha, Nebraska. She debuted at age thirteen in a local production of *A Kiss for Cinderella*. Her leading man was a family friend who had just made a name for himself on Broadway—Henry Fonda.

Dorothy did a season of stock and then set off to conquer Broadway. "It never occurred to me that I might not make it," she admitted recently. "I meant to be a hit in a hit." She understudied Martha Scott in *Our Town* (1938) and then took over the role. She was then opposite John Barrymore in *My Dear Children*. The next year she achieved her goal in *Claudia* (1941).

Dorothy got off to an impressive start in Hollywood. She proved as charming in the film version of *Claudia* (1943) as she had been on Broadway. She made the memorable *A Tree Grows in Brooklyn* (1945) and the thriller *The Spiral Staircase* (1946), both hits critically and at the box office. Her producer David O. Selznick was so pleased he gave her a new convertible.

But Dorothy McGuire's character did not lend itself to the obligations of an actress under contract. She would not be glamorized nor would she date actors. One of the roles she turned down was *Anna and the King of Siam*. Her refusal to wear grotesque makeup for *The Enchanted Cottage* (1945) proved correct but it made her no friends. Dorothy was adamant about keeping her personal life private. The one complaint never made about her was that she couldn't act. Her performance in *Gentleman's Agreement* (1947) brought her an Oscar nomination.

Her qualities were very special ones and while she continued to make pictures the parts she began receiving were not ones which earn accolades in Hollywood. She drifted quickly from young star to leading lady to character actress.

Her movies include: *Invitation* (1952), *Three Coins in the Fountain* (1954), *Friendly Persuasion* (1956), *A Summer Place* (1959), and *The Dark at the Top of the Stairs* (1960).

Since 1943 Dorothy has been married to the wealthy John Swope. They have a teenage son and a daughter Topo who has appeared in a few films including *Hot Rock*. The Swopes' Beverly Hills mansion which once belonged to Corinne Griffith [2] is filled with blow-ups of her husband's prize-winning photos. Their neighbor is Randolph Scott.[2]

During a rare interview she recently dispelled the myth that she had lost interest in her career: "My husband and I travel a great deal and when I'm home I've many things which I like to do. But I love to make pictures and it would be nice to do something on Broadway again. I don't think about acting very much because if I did I would miss it more than I care to."

Dorothy McGuire and Richard Lamparski chat in the actress's Beverly Hills home. *(Shelly Davis)*

In 1940 the Dutch actor was under contract to Universal Pictures. *(Ray Jones)*

PHILIP DORN

The leading man of 1940s Hollywood films was born Hein Van Der Niet on September 30, 1901, in Scheveningen, Netherlands. He was the youngest of nine children in a very poor family. His parents were deeply religious and strongly disapproved of his acting ambitions. But by his late teens he was playing leads on the Dutch stage under the name Fritz van Dongen. Then for a while he made quite a success in a magic act as Ben Abbas wearing a turban and Indian makeup.

The playwright Jan Fabricius took an interest in him and in 1929 sent Dorn on a tour of all the Dutch colonies playing a wide variety of roles. He began making motion pictures and by the mid-thirties Philip was a matinee idol in Europe. Two of his pictures which are still shown in Europe are *The Tiger of Eschnafuer* (1938) and *The Indian Tomb* (1938).

One of his directors, Henry Koster, had become established in Hollywood and sent for Dorn in 1939. He signed a contract with Universal but was used mainly on loan-outs. Neither Universal nor M-G-M where he went for six years gave him the star treatment. Still his stage training and rich voice made impressions on audiences—particularly women. He projected strength, good judgment, and kindness.

What probably held him back in Hollywood was his refusal to play the involved games of studio politics. He found Louis B. Mayer ridiculous and did not hesitate to return his unpleasant remarks. Mayer had his revenge by refusing to allow Philip to do either *Watch on the Rhine* or *Jacobowsky and the Colonel* on Broadway.

He debuted on American screens in *Escape* (1940). Some of his others are: *Underground* (1941), *Paris After Dark* (1943), *Passage to Marseilles* (1944), *I've Always Loved You* (1946) with Catherine McLeod (married to actor Don Keefer and living in Sherman Oaks; she writes for fan magazines under various names), and *The Fighting Kentuckian* (1949).

Dorn is an actor of the old school and has always found Hollywood stars and their behavior somewhat absurd. His refusal to take Joan Crawford seriously caused endless trouble when they made *Reunion* (1942) together. All of their love scenes had to be re-dubbed.

Throughout his life he had been plagued by phlebitis. Then in 1945 he suffered the first of a series of strokes. He recovered from each but in 1955 received a minor concussion in a freak accident while playing *The Fourposter* in The Hague. Although he has regained his faculties he refuses to chance a role. He politely but firmly turned down *The Andersonville Trial* on Broadway and the role of Anne Frank's father in the movie.

Dorn sees none of his contemporaries and never watches his pictures on TV. He restricts his activities to his library and to walking and playing with his German shepherd. He and his wife Marianne van Dam, who was a well-known singer and actress in Europe, live in a pretty house in Westwood, California. It is one of their many real estate properties. He speaks and walks with some hesitation but his condition has in no way impaired his sharp sense of humor.

Dorn in the yard of his Westwood, California, home. *(Albert Laurey)*

In 1943 Margo was under contract to RKO Radio Pictures.

MARGO

The screen and stage star was born Marie Marguerita Guadalupe Teresa Estela Bolado Castilla y O'Donnell in Mexico City on May 10, 1918. She was coached by Eduardo Casino, Rita Hayworth's father, and began dancing professionally when she was nine years old. Her aunt was then married to Xavier Cugat who was not yet well known. When Margo was twelve years old she began dancing with his band at Agua Caliente. The Waldorf Astoria brought them both to New York. It was from that engagement that Cugat clicked in the United States. The Rumba he played and which Margo danced became a craze. Charles MacArthur and Ben Hecht felt she had the special quality they wanted for the female lead in their movie *Crime Without Passion* (1934). In spite of the splash she made in it Hollywood didn't really get excited about her until she did *Winterset* (1935) on Broadway. Even then, though her notices were excellent, RKO would not let her play the part in the screen version until she tested.

Her looks and voice were very individual and were most effective as the girl who ages to an old woman in *Lost Horizon* (1937). Studio chief Harry Cohn wanted Rita Hayworth for the part but director Frank Capra insisted on Margo. It was 1969 before she ever saw the film.

Some of her other pictures were: *Miracle on Main Street* (1940), *The Leopard Man* (1943), *Viva Zapata* (1952), *I'll Cry Tomorrow* (1955), and *Who's Got the Action?* (1962).

After doing *Masque of Kings* (1937) on Broadway she married Francis Lederer.[4] They were divorced in 1940. In 1944 she was back on Broadway in *A Bell for Adano*.

On December 6, 1945, she became Mrs. Eddie Albert. They live in a large Spanish house with a view of the Sierra Madre in Pacific Palisades. It was once owned by Billie Dove [2] who now lives next door.

After her second marriage Margo devoted her considerable energies to raising her two children. Until recently she conducted acting classes. One of her pupils is now a movie star—Edward Albert, her son. The Alberts also have an adopted daughter. She does not rule out working again in films or on the stage if the part excites her.

She is a key figure in the Chicano Cultural Center, Plaza de la Raza, in Los Angeles.

Margo and her husband Eddie Albert live next door to Billie Dove in Pacific Palisades, California. *(Michael Knowles)*

In 1937 Michael Whalen was under contract to Twentieth Century-Fox.

MICHAEL WHALEN

The debonair leading man of stage and movies was born Joseph Shovlin on June 30, 1902, in Wilkes Barre, Pennsylvania. His first interest was the piano but he stopped playing when he was seventeen and joined the staff of the Woolworth chain. By the time he resigned at age twenty-three he had become a manager of one of their dime stores.

Michael started out to tour the world but only got as far as New York City where he caught a matinee performance of *The Cradle Song* (1927). He forgot about his travel plans and signed on as an apprentice with Eva Le Gallienne's acting group. He debuted as a 75-year-old man.

To supplement his income Whalen modeled a great deal for the famed artist James Montgomery Flagg, posing even as old women.

He came to Hollywood in 1933 without prospects but immediately landed the role of the Dauphin in the Pasadena Playhouse production of *When Knighthood Was in Flower*. Then he did *Common Flesh* at a local theatre and consequently received bids to act for the Schuberts and make movies for Fox. He chose the latter and made his first picture, *Professional Soldier* (1935), with the late Victor McLaughlin. He remembers the star as being "unbelievably rude and coarse." He made quite a few films with Gloria Stuart but has nothing good to say about her either as an actress or as a person.

Whalen's two really important features, *Poor Little Rich Girl* (1936) and *Wee Willie Winkie* (1937), both starred Shirley Temple. He has only the highest praise for the moppet superstar. His stage training and good looks gave a measure of class to such otherwise unimportant movies such as: *The Country Doctor* (1936) with the Dionne Quintuplets,[3] *Time Out for Murder* (1938) with Chick Chandler (living in Laguna Beach, California), *Ellery Queen, Master Detective* (1940), *Nazi Agent* (1942), and *Wild Weed* (1949) with the late Robert Kent. He played Jack London heroes in *White Fang* (1936) and *Sign of the Wolf* (1941).

Michael starred on Broadway for two years in *Ten Little Indians* (1944) and then went with the thriller on a lengthy road tour.

Most of the work he did in the late forties and fifties was in stock. In 1960 he made his movie swan song *Elmer Gantry* and in 1964 did a guest shot on *My Three Sons*.

Whalen is very outspoken as to why his career did not pan out as well as many expected. "It was because I was an anti-Communist long before anyone ever heard of Joe McCarthy," he allowed recently. "It wasn't that I was so brave. I just never realized what power those Red bastards had in this town." He is equally conservative about his religion and is confused and resentful about the changes in the Roman Catholic Church.

He was once engaged to Ilona Massey [1] who is the only contemporary he sees from the old days. Whalen, who is still a bachelor, shared his home with his mother until she died several years ago. He now lives with a friend who is also a former actor. Most of his time is spent gardening around his homes in the San Fernando Valley and the interior of Mexico.

Michael Whalen's Encino, California, home is filled with antiques. *(Martitia Palmer)*

In 1932 Heather signed a contract in Hollywood with Fox Films.

HEATHER ANGEL

The ethereal English actress was born on February 9, 1909, in Oxford where her father was a chemistry professor. At sixteen she left school to attend the London Polytechnic of Dramatic Arts. By 1926 she was a member of the Old Vic where she played small parts in Shakespeare.

Heather made something of a name for herself in the lead of *A Christmas Eve* and then toured Great Britain, Egypt, and the Orient with a repertory company.

When the star of *The City of Song* (1932) refused to dye her hair Heather replaced her, making her movie debut opposite the late Jan Kipeura.

Fox Films became aware of her from the English film *The Hound of the Baskervilles* (1932) and she was placed under contract. She was with the studio for two years before going to Universal. Both lots were in the midst of corporate shake-ups at the time and the pictures she made did little to further her career. Two examples are: *Charlie Chan's Greatest Case* (1933) and *Springtime for Henry* (1934).

She got some good pictures such as: *The Informer* (1935), *The Last of the Mohicans* (1936), *Pride and Prejudice* (1940), *That Hamilton Woman* (1941), and *Lifeboat* (1944). But the studios continued to think of her as being "a little too special" and her fate was usually either costume films like *The Three Musketeers* (1935) or the Bulldog Drummond series of which she did five. In 1941 she made an interesting B film *Singapore Woman* with Brenda Marshall (divorced from William Holden and living in Palm Springs), Virginia Field (Mrs. Willard Parker of Palm Desert, California), and Rose Hobart (a Religious Science practitioner in

Sherman Oaks, California). She admits to being disappointed when she tested but failed to win the role of Melanie in *Gone With The Wind* and the role eventually played by Elizabeth Taylor in *National Velvet.* "I had a strong drive," she said recently, "but it was to be a fine actress—not a star."

She does not enjoy seeing herself on the screen and feels she has never had a single part she could really get her teeth into. Heather was on Broadway briefly in *The Wooky* (1941). From 1934 to 1942 she was married to the late Ralph Forbes.

Her career waned during the 1950s. She was one of the voices of *Peter Pan* (1953) and turned up in the shocker *Premature Burial* (1962). She has done occasional roles on the *Mr. Novak* and *A Family Affair* TV series, but is not anxious to work steadily and will accept nothing that contains violence.

In 1951 Heather and her second husband, Robert B. Sinclair, moved to Santa Barbara. He directed such Broadway plays as *Philadelphia Story* and *Pride and Prejudice.* In 1970 he was stabbed to death by an intruder while Heather looked on helplessly.

Heather Angel lives alone now on a hill overlooking the Pacific Ocean in Montecito, California. She keeps two horses and does a lot of riding and swimming.

Heather Angel is living alone these days in a house on a hill in Montecito, a section of Santa Barbara, California. (*Jerry Beirne*)

From left to right: Art Van Harvey played Vic Gook, Clarence Hartzell was Uncle Fletcher, Bernadine Flynn was Sade, and Billy Idelson played their adopted son Rush. *(Paul M. Rhymer Collection)*

VIC AND SADE

At 8:30 A.M. on June 29, 1932, Chicago radio station WNAQ broadcast the first episode of a radio series that at its peak had over seven million regular listeners. Over three decades after it went off the air there is still a *Vic and Sade* cult all over North America. A two-hour recorded tribute to the show was aired by a number of U.S. radio stations in 1973 and brought thousands of requests for taped copies.

Its humor was so unique and its style so underplayed that it was recognized even in its heyday as being a significant contribution to genuine American humor. Hendrik van Loon said it was the greatest piece of Americana being produced at that time. It used to receive almost monthly fan letters from a New York State judge. Today's acknowledged expert on *Vic and Sade* is the actor Tony Randall, who can recite entire fifteen-minute shows.

Usually only four characters were heard: Vic Gook and his wife Sade, their adopted son Rush (who joined the cast shortly after it debuted), and Uncle Fletcher, who was a much later addition. Much of their conversation centered on their friends and neighbors. There was Ruthie Stembottom who used to accompany Sade to the washrag sales at Yamelton's and Y. Y. Flirtch who was forever getting hit by fast passenger trains. He worked as an armed guard at the Ohio State Home for the Bald. Rush often went down to watch the fat men play handball at the Y along with his chums Smelly Clark or Blue Tooth Johnson. Vic was employed by the Consolidated Kitchenware Company and was the Exalted Big Dipper in the Drousy Venus Chapter of the Sacred Stars of the Milky Way. Sade often would "yoo-hoo" to Mr. Gumpox, their garbage man, who had

186

a horse named Howard. Beef Punkles were often on the Gook's menu for supper.

Their title was "Radio's Home Folks" and their theme was "Chanson Bohémienne." The show was broadcast five days a week for two and a half years. Then Crisco picked it up and was its sponsor almost to the last broadcast on September 29, 1944.

The players were always the late Art Van Harvey and Bernadine Flynn (widowed and living in Clay City, Illinois) in the title roles. Uncle Fletcher was Clarence Hartzell (retired and living in West Dundee, Illinois). Rush was played by Bill Idelson (the producer and writer of such TV shows as *Love American Style* and *The Bob Newhart Show*).

Some other Vic and Sadisms: Rishigan Fishigan of Sishigan, Michigan, who married Jane Bane from Payne, Maine; the identical twins Robert and Slobert Hink; Four-Fisted Frank Fuddleman; the Bright Kentucky Hotel and the Little Tiny Petite Feathered Pheasant Tea Shoppe.

A compilation of the *Vic and Sade* scripts, *The Small House Halfway Up in the Next Block,* was published in 1972 by Rhymer's widow.

Paul M. Rhymer took the boredom and banality of everyday life in a small Midwestern town, combined it with his sense of the ridiculous, and produced a show that was in no way derivative. It is so respected within the radio and TV industry that no one has ever dared to parody it, much less imitate it.

In 1940 Edgar Guest, another of its ardent fans, wrote a tribute that is still true today: "No building human hands have made, Could hold the friends of *Vic and Sade*."

Bill Idelson and one of his three sons, Jonathan. *(Ene Riisna)*

Below, right: Sade in Clay City, Illinois. *(Jack Foster)*

Uncle Fletcher today. *(Don Koll)*

In 1935 Gene Raymond signed a long-term contract with RKO Pictures.

GENE RAYMOND

The handsome star of stage and screen was born Raymond Guion on August 13, 1908, in New York City. He attended Professional Children's School and made his Broadway debut in *The Piper* (1920). Through his roles in *Why Not?* (1922), *Cradle Snatchers* (1925), and *Take My Advice* (1927) with Genevieve Tobin [4] he earned the title "the nearly perfect juvenile." His later credits include *The War Song* (1928) and *Young Sinners* (1929).

His name was changed to Gene Raymond when he began his screen career in *Personal Maid* (1931). It was followed by *Red Dust* (1932), *Zoo in Budapest* (1933), *Seven Keys to Baldpate* (1935), *Life of the Party* (1937), and *Cross-Country Romance* (1940).

After spending World War II as a bomber pilot he was discharged as a major and returned to the screen in *The Locket* (1946) with Laraine Day. [3] He directed as well as starred in *Million Dollar Weekend* (1948) but it was unsuccessful. He has only been in a few movies since: *Hit the Deck* (1955) and *The Best Man* (1964).

Some of Gene's leading ladies were: Barbara Stanwyck, Jean Harlow, Bette Davis, Olympe Bradna (married and living in Carmel, California) Loretta Young, and the late Nancy Carroll. In *Sadie McKee* (1934) he sang "All I Do Is Dream of You" to Joan Crawford. But the star he is most closely associated with is Jeannette MacDonald with whom he made *Smilin' Through* (1941). Their wedding on June 16, 1937, was the biggest Hollywood had seen since the late Rod La Rocque and Vilma Banky's (living in Beverly Hills) a decade earlier. Police held back an estimated 15,000 fans outside the church which held almost every name in filmdom. There were one million roses. The late Harold Lloyd, Johnny Mack Brown,[3] and Basil Rathbone ushered. The bridesmaids included Ginger Rogers and Fay Wray.[2] Nelson Eddy was the soloist. They honeymooned on Hawaii with another pair of newlyweds, Mary Pickford and Buddy Rogers,[3] before moving into their Bel-Aire mansion, Twin Gables. They became, and remained until Miss MacDonald's death in 1965, one of moviedom's most glamorous and popular couples.

An astute businessman, Raymond has done very well financially and still has a hand in real estate and the stock market. When he went on strike from his studio for two years in 1938 he wrote songs which his wife introduced in her concerts. The two packed houses across the country when they toured in *The Guardsman* (1951). He was active on TV as a host of *Fireside Theatre* in 1953 and acted through the early sixties. Gene still makes an occasional appearance.

He has never remarried and remains active in the Hollywood social scene among the Old Guard. For a time he was the constant companion of Jane Wyman. Raymond holds strong opinions on the trend movies have taken and is conservative politically. He lives in a large modern building just off Wilshire Boulevard in Westwood in an apartment which houses his large Lincolniana collection.

Gene is very much a part of Hollywood's Old Guard social scene. *(Jon Virzi)*

By 1945 Kurt Kreuger was a familiar
face to American moviegoers.

KURT KREUGER

The handsome blond movie actor was born on July 23, 1916. Contrary
to studio publicity during World War II which had him for a while
a Swiss ski instructor and at another time a Dutch student, he was born
in Michenberg, Germany, and brought up in St. Moritz, Switzerland.
Kurt's German father disapproved of his son's wanderlust and interest in
acting. For a while Kreuger attended the University of London's School
of Economics and then transferred to Columbia University in New York
City. When he dropped his studies his allowance was cut off and in 1939
he took a job as a travel agent and enrolled with the Provincetown
Players on Cape Cod. By 1941 he had landed a small part in *Candle in the
Wind* on Broadway with Helen Hayes and understudied one of the leads.

Kreuger made his movie debut in a small part in *Edge of Darkness*
(1943) and did bits in *Action in the North Atlantic* (1943), and *Un-
conquered* (1947). During his six years under contract to Twentieth
Century-Fox he made: *The Strange Death of Adolph Hitler* (1943), *Sahara*
(1943), *None Shall Escape* (1944), *Paris Underground* (1945), *The Spider*
(1945) with Cara Williams (married to a Beverly Hills real estate broker).
He escaped being typecast as a Nazi through roles in *Sentimental Journey*
(1946) and *Unfaithfully Yours* (1948).

In 1949 after a quarrel with his studio he walked out on his contract
and went to Europe where he made quite a few German films in which
he played the lead, something that always eluded him in Hollywood.

After a very serious auto accident in 1955 he returned to the United States. He had become a citizen in 1944.

Kurt made *The Enemy Below* (1957), *Legion of the Doomed* (1958), and *The St. Valentine's Day Massacre* (1967) but his career never caught fire again. One severe disappointment came when Marlon Brando got the role he wanted so much in *The Young Lions*.

He has a fine singing voice and was seriously considered for the original Broadway cast of *The Sound of Music*. The reason he wasn't used was that he didn't look old enough to be the father of seven children. He was so flattered he didn't mind at all.

Kreuger may not have become a star but he has a consolation in living like one in a Beverly Hills mansion and driving a Rolls Royce. He has never married and lives with his German shepherd Rolfe. He follows the ski season around the world and occasionally sees Helmut Dantine with whom he made *Hotel Berlin* (1945) and *Escape in the Desert* (1945).

His money is invested in luxury homes which he rents to luminaries such as Darryl F. Zanuck and Gloria Swanson.

Kurt explained his attitude toward his career in a recent interview: "I like doing something now and then but the part must appeal to my ego or my bank account. So when you see Kreuger on the screen you can be sure he's either got a very juicy part or he's being paid a hell of a lot of money."

Today Kurt is much involved in real estate. *(Don Lynn)*

In 1944 Darryl was in *Song of Russia*.

DARRYL HICKMAN

The child actor was born in Los Angeles on July 28, 1930. His mother, who had wanted a career herself, named him after Darryl F. Zanuck. She enrolled him in dancing class when he was three and a half years old. By the time he was four Darryl was a Meglin Kiddie and soon afterward began working in pictures as an extra and then a bit player.

He got two big breaks at once when Bing Crosby picked him for a featured part in his movie *The Star Maker* (1939). At the same time he was signed up by Crosby's brother Everett who was an agent. Darryl never became a star but he had good parts in some important films: *Grapes of Wrath* (1940), *Men of Boystown* (1941), *The Human Comedy* (1943), *Kiss and Tell* (1945), *Two Years Before the Mast* (1946), *Submarine Command* (1951), and *Tea and Sympathy* (1956).

He got most of his schooling on movie lots and is still aware of the gaps in his education. He liked the pretend part of acting but disliked some of his contemporaries like Butch Jenkins [3] whom he has described as "the most miserable kid I've ever known." Darryl used to play football with Elizabeth Taylor. She was his very first date. Peggy Ann Garner [3] was another.

He was in a seminary briefly in 1951 with the intention of becoming a Passionist priest.

His younger brother Dwayne had never been pushed by Mrs. Hickman as Darryl was but developed an acting ambition on his own. When he made a name on TV via his part on *The Bob Cummings Show* in the early 1950s Darryl was delighted for him. But when he became a star with his own series *Dobie Gillis* in 1959 there began a period of subtle but strong rivalry between the two. Both careers faded in the early sixties. Today the brothers are friendly but quite different in personality. Dwayne retired completely to run his own public relations firm in Las Vegas for a while. After a costly divorce in 1972 he returned to Hollywood and is again available for acting assignments.

Darryl feels he was psychologically a child until he was in his thirties and matured only through analysis. His last acting job was in the title role of *George M* in 1970. He thinks it was the best work he ever did.

He had already written and sold several teleplays when he joined CBS-TV as an associate producer. He is now Executive Producer for Daytime Programming in the network's New York offices.

Darryl will not allow either of his two sons to act until they are on their own. "I feel I missed a childhood," he said recently, "and there's no substitute for that."

He recently asked his mother for the first time why at the age of four and a half he was acting in movies. "Because, darling," replied Mrs. Hickman, "that is what you had always wanted."

Darryl in his office at CBS-TV in New York City with the author's associate, Michael Knowles. *(Sylvia Brodsky)*

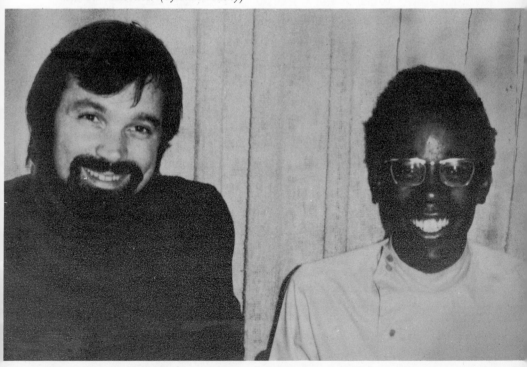

Gail played the Annie Oakley role on television from 1953 to 1960.

GAIL DAVIS

TV's Annie Oakley was born Betty Jeanne Grayson on October 5, 1925, in Little Rock, Arkansas. At age two she was chosen "Arkansas' Most Beautiful Baby." While at the University of Texas she was picked as one of the "Blue Bonnet Belles" and later when she attended Harkum Junior College the fraternity houses at nearby University of Pennsylvania named her their Queen.

In 1945 Gail married an army captain who aspired to acting. After his discharge in 1946 the couple came to Hollywood. She was exercising on the roof of their hotel one day when she was approached by John Carroll [4] and his agent who took her to M-G-M. She was under contract to the Culver City lot only long enough to make *The Romance of Rosy Ridge* (1947) and *Merton of the Movies* (1947). Then Gail went to RKO for *If You Knew Susie* (1948) and *Overland Telegraph* (1951) with the late Tim Holt.[2] She went to Republic for *The Far Frontier* (1949) when Dale Evans became pregnant and was unable to co-star with Roy Rogers.

Cow Town (1950) kicked off her long association with Gene Autry.[1] She co-starred in a series of his features: *Whirlwind* (1951) and *Texans Never Cry* (1951).

It was television and her role of Annie Oakley that brought her stardom. For seven straight years beginning in 1953 Gail turned out thirty-minute black and white segments which Autry produced. She was the niece of the sheriff who only appeared in the first episode. After that he always seemed to be out of town leaving things to Annie and his deputy, Lofty Craig, who was played by Brad Johnson. Annie had a brother Tagg who was forever stumbling into trouble. The role was played by Jimmy Hawkins who later turned up as the love interest on the *Donna Reed Show*. He is now in the producing end of films.

While Annie was "the gal with the gun," the show's scripters were careful to keep her soft and, as the character might say, "right friendly." It was her marksmanship that was usually featured and Gail did it all herself. She disarmed and wounded the bad guys but never killed anyone. Although she is an excellent horsewoman, when the plots called for dangerous trick rides she was always doubled by Donna Hall.

Gail loved filming her shows although they didn't make her rich. When the series went into re-runs she and her famous horse Target toured for several years in rodeos and fairs. By the time she presented herself back in Hollywood for work she was hopelessly typecast and now too old for the part of the cowboy's girl.

She lives in Toluca Lake, California, with her third husband, an auto executive. Her one daughter is a college student. Gail is a partner in a personal management firm which handles such personalities as Janis Paige and Mel Torme.

While never much of an actress, she gave Annie a great deal of warmth and had a genuine quality that both boys and girls responded to. Her sponsors were surprised that so many adults watched the show but what amazed Gail was the letters of proposal she received from pre-adolescent boys. Not all of their proposals were of marriage.

Although she likes what she's doing now she also admits that it would be nice to act again. She hastens to add however that "it would have to be something that wouldn't mar Annie's image."

Gail is a partner now in a personal management firm in Hollywood. *(Brian Gari)*

Kirk Alyn appearing as Superman in the famous serial.

KIRK ALYN

The serial king was born in Oxford, New Jersey, on October 8, 1910.

Kirk was on Broadway as early as 1930 as a chorus boy in *Girl Crazy*. He toured with Olson & Johnson in the mid-thirties and then joined a company headed by the late band leader George Olsen, doing a comedy routine with Imogene Coca.

Alyn worked quite often in small parts in both A's and B's but never really clicked. He was seen briefly in *Lucky Jordan* (1942), *Overland Mail Robbery* (1943), *Forty Thieves* (1944), and *Sweet Genevieve* (1947) with Jimmy Lydon.[4]

At one point Republic Pictures was interested in him as the lead for a series of westerns, but his agent insisted there were "bigger things" in store for him. Shortly afterward he was offered the title role in *Superman* (1948), a serial based on the comic strip hero. Aside from being somewhat amused by how seriously the producers treated the character he thought of it as just another job. He was not allowed to appear off the set in his Superman uniform which at no time was to be referred to as a "costume." There also was an exceptionally strict morals clause in his contract. One thing that bothered him from the start was that he was billed only as playing Clark Kent, Superman's alter-ego, a mild-mannered reporter for the Metropolis *Daily Planet*.

The serial was booked into the RKO first-run theatre chain and opened the day schools let out for the summer. Alyn knew the serial was a hit with the kids as soon as it was released. It didn't occur to him until much later that it would severely limit his career. When he signed to do the second series, *Atom Man vs. Superman* (1950), he insisted on twice as much money only because of the extreme rigors of the part. He had lost 17 pounds making the first.

His Lois Lane in both serials was Noel Neill (single and living in the Santa Monica Canyon). The director was Spencer Bennet (living in Hollywood), the dean of serial directors.

The first time Kirk heard a casting director greet him "Hello, Superman" he knew his professional fate was sealed. They explained that directors and producers simply felt anyone so closely identified with *Superman* would be distracting in another part. He did manage to make other serials: *Daughter of Don Q.* (1946) with Adrian Booth (married to David Brian and living in Sherman Oaks), *Federal Agents vs. Underworld, Inc.* (1949) with Rosemary La Planche, *Radar Patrol vs. Spy King* (1950), and *Blackhawk* (1952).

He turned down a large sum of money to do the TV *Superman* series of the 1950s and the part went to the late George Reeves. Instead he worked in stock and road companies and did occasional TV and feature jobs.

From 1943 to 1949 he was married to Virginia O'Brien [4] by whom he has three children.

The man whom *Variety* once described as "the best known unknown actor in Hollywood" is one of the biggest draws in the nostalgia business and is in constant demand at conventions. He has written his own book on his experiences playing the man from the planet Krypton; this book is entitled *A Job for Superman,* and Alyn published it himself.

Alyn never remarried. He lives in a home he built on the Arizona side of Lake Havasu which has a view of the London Bridge.

Kirk and his son Johnny, whose mother is Virginia O'Brien. (*Paul Schaffer*)

In 1948 she was the star of *Liltin'
Martha Tilton Time* over NBC
Radio. *(NBC)*

MARTHA TILTON

The singer of the Big Band Era known as the "Liltin' Miss Martha Tilton"
was born in Corpus Christie, Texas, on November 14, 1915. Her parents
played the piano and sang a great deal at home. The Tiltons moved to
Los Angeles when Martha was seven months old. In her early teens
after some coaxing from her friends she sang to the accompaniment of a
small group at a party. They asked her to join them when they played
on a local radio station. She only did it for fun but was asked to stay
on as a regular. She was, however, never paid.

An agent heard her on the air and got her a booking at the Coconut
Grove singing with Al Lippan's band. Then she toured for two years
with Hal Grayson's aggregation before becoming the distaff member of
"3 Hits and a Miss." That group was joined by several other singers,
among them Jo Stafford (married to Paul Weston and living in Beverly
Hills) to form a swing chorus for Benny Goodman's radio show. When
Goodman's girl singer left, Martha got the job and over the next three
and a half years of one-nighters, radio programs, and recording sessions
became quite a name. Martha also found time to appear in four movies:
Sunny (1941), *Swing Hostess* (1944), *Crime, Inc.* (1945) in which she gave
an exceptionally good performance, and *The Benny Goodman Story* (1956).

When she left Goodman NBC showcased her for several seasons on her
own radio program. Beginning in 1951 she and Curt Massey (living in

Palm Springs) began an eight-year stint for Alka-Selzer over CBS Radio. Then they did another five years again with Country Washburn's Orchestra on NBC-TV. When that went off the air in 1964 Martha retired so completely she doesn't even sing around the house.

Although she has no gold records, Martha cut a few big hits: "I'll Walk Alone," "How Are Things in Glocca Mora," "Time After Time," and "And the Angels Sing."

She has fond memories of the Swing Era but doesn't miss it one bit. During one two-year period at the height of her career she had only one day off. She summed up her feelings in a recent interview: "I'm very grateful for what happened to me. I was well paid for what I loved doing most—singing." Although she likes hearing from fans and contemporaries Martha never initiates the reunions. She and her three children have an excellent rapport on the new sounds in music but they seem quite uninterested in their mother's career. Says Martha with a laugh, "Sometimes it kind of bugs me that they're not more impressed."

She and her husband, an aerospace executive with North American-Rockwell, live in Los Angeles' Mandeville Canyon with their teenage daughter, in a home with a swimming pool and tennis court. Two days after they were married in 1953 her husband, then a test pilot, picked her up, stumbled, and broke Martha's leg. The story broke every newscast and paper in the country with the theme "Martha Tilton breaks leg on wedding night."

Martha leads a happy life now in the Mandeville Canyon area of West Los Angeles. *(Jerry Mastroli)*

In the 1950s Jimmy was the most controversial and one of the best-looking baseball players in the major leagues. *(United Press Photo)*

JIMMY PIERSALL

The baseball player who became as famous for his behavior as for his game was born November 14, 1929, in Waterbury, Connecticut. His late father was determined that Jimmy would be a star athlete and trained him relentlessly at hitting, running, and fielding. Once when his son fell during a skating contest the elder Piersall suffered a heart attack.

Before joining the Boston Red Sox in 1949 Jimmy made quite a name for himself in high school basketball.

At first with the Red Sox he played well, teased his teammates, and led fans in cheers for himself. But it wasn't long before the fear of failure instilled in him by his father made him crack. He once squirted home plate with a water pistol so the umpire could see it better. Another time he hit a home run and then ran the bases backward.

Piersall was thought by some to be the greatest center fielder in American League history. Casey Stengel called him the best defensive right fielder he had ever seen. One sports writer named Jimmy's knack for stealing bases "homer-cide." He had at least a dozen catches that bordered on the extraordinary. But it was his antics that made the headlines of sports pages. More and more he was becoming irrational until his temper was turned even toward his own teammates. He engaged in fistfights with both

Jim Bunning and Moose Skowron. In 1952 Piersall was placed in the violent ward of a mental hospital.

His painfully frank autobiography *Fear Strikes Out* (1955) described the anguish he felt and won him admirers who had no interest in baseball itself.

It was some time, however, before some sports fans forgave him for admitting his weaknesses. As late as the 1960s when he was a Detroit Tiger Jimmy was regularly taunted from the bleachers with insults. One man yelled "crazy, crazy, crazy" through 18 innings of a double header.

He moved from the diamond to the front office of the Los Angeles Angels in 1968. With all of his difficulties he had averaged a batting average throughout his career of .272.

Jimmy lives with his second wife in Arlington, Texas. Of his nine children one son is doing very well in basketball and another is a hockey player.

Although the 1957 movie version of his book was a critical success Piersall thought it was "terrible." He had a strong personal dislike of Tony Perkins who played him.

Jimmy says his well-deserved reputation helps him get his foot in the door as Group Sales and Promotion Director for the Texas Rangers. "People want to meet me and see if I'm really as fiery and brash as they've heard." He is.

Piersall now does a lot of public speaking in his job with the Texas Rangers baseball team.

In 1939 Anne Shirley was one of the brightest stars on the RKO lot.

ANNE SHIRLEY

The movie star who walked away from it all when she was at the very top was born Dawn Evelyneen Paris on April 17, 1919, in New York City. By the time she was eighteen months old her father had died and her mother had gotten her work modeling baby clothes. Then she began getting parts in silents such as *The Miracle Child* (1923) with Dustin Farnum.

Mrs. Paris brought Dawn to Hollywood and she appeared in Pola Negri's *The Spanish Dancer* (1923) under the name Dawn O'Day. She played Madge Bellamy (single and living in Ontario, California), Janet Gaynor,[2] and Myrna Loy as babies. Still they were barely making ends meet. But the harder things got the more determined her mother was to see her daughter get that one big break. It came when the late Mitzi Green, at the time RKO's top young star, became difficult and was replaced in the plum role of *Anne of Green Gables* (1934). Upon the picture's completion Dawn O'Day became Anne Shirley. Upon its release Anne Shirley became a star.

Her position on the popularity polls of the time and her pleasant disposition made Anne the fair-haired girl of the lot. On her seventeenth birthday the studio gave her a new car. She was dimpled and seemed unaffected but it was a certain shy quality that brought her a multitude of fans. She made *Chasing Yesterday* (1935), *Chatterbox* (1936), *Mother Carey's Chickens* (1938), *Career* (1939), *Saturday's Children* (1940), *All That Money Can Buy* (1941), *The Powers Girl* (1942), and *Murder, My Sweet* (1944).

In 1937 Anne was probably the most envied girl in America. She played Laurel to Barbara Stanwyck's memorable *Stella Dallas,* and married one of the most handsome young actors on the screen, John Payne.[3] Their daughter Julie is now an actress. After a second marriage to producer Adrian Scott failed she became the wife of Charles Lederer. He was the scenarist of such pictures as *His Girl Friday, Comrade X,* and *Can-Can.* A renowned wit, at the peak of his career her husband was one of Hollywood's most prized social catches. He is also the nephew of Marion Davies and one of her heirs. The Lederers have one son.

The couple spend part of each week in their large Beverly Hills home and the rest in a two-story Malibu Beach house right on the Pacific Ocean. Anne has filled it with bright colors and her many cats.

At the age of twenty-five, with her career thriving, she retired and has not even considered a part since then. Recently she explained why: "My mother wanted me to be a star so she could say she was Anne Shirley's mother. Well, I became one and now we're both happy. They were wonderful years but I did it all for her. To tell you the truth I never think about my career except that I often feel grateful that it has brought me such a good life."

Anne divides her time between her Beverly Hills estate and her beach house in Malibu. *(Frank Edwards)*

Barbara Jo appeared in a costume as Vera Vague only for publicity stills (left). At broadcasts she was always smartly dressed. (*NBC Radio*)

"VERA VAGUE"
Barbara Jo Allen

The actress who became nationally famous by the character she created was born on Fifth Avenue in New York City on September 2. She appeared in almost every play produced by her high school. After studying at the Sorbonne in Paris, Barbara Jo returned to New York City determined to support herself as an actress. Shortly afterward the second of her parents died and she moved to Los Angeles to live with an uncle.

One of her first parts was in 1937 when she played Beth Holly on Carlton E. Morse's [4] *One Man's Family*. After that she worked steadily on radio on such programs as *Death Valley Days* and *I Love a Mystery*.

The character that brought her fame and a considerable amount of money was inspired when she watched a woman lecturing a P.T.A. group on world literature. "She had absolutely no continuity of thought," said Barbara Jo recently. "I listened to her change the subject with every sentence she spoke and I knew I had her down pat." Although she has worked very little in the last two decades, Vera Vague is still a household phrase to millions of Americans.

Barbara was first heard as Vera in 1939 on *NBC Matinee*. She became almost at once a radio counterpart of the American clubwoman whom the late cartoonist Helen Hokinson caricatured in magazines throughout the 1930s and 1940s. Vera, like her name, was indeed vague. But by writing her own material Barbara Jo made her very vivid in the minds of radio listeners.

Bob Hope hired her for his Pepsodent radio show and she remained with him for many years. During World War II she along with Jerry Colonna [3] and Frances Langford [2] toured U.S. service installations around the world.

Even though she appeared in 39 feature films Barbara Jo is very closely identified in the minds of professionals as Vera Vague. Most radio listeners know only the character and have no idea who played her. The main reason she retired is that she grew weary of the part and resented the limitations it had placed on her career.

One of the most disconcerting things about the role was that studio audiences were convulsed as soon as she appeared before a microphone. The ridiculousness of Vera Vague made people laugh even though Barbara Jo was an attractive and exceptionally well-dressed woman.

In 1943 she married Norman Morrell, who was then Bob Hope's producer. He is now with Andy Williams. They live in a large home which is right on the Pacific Ocean in Santa Barbara. Barbara Jo has made 34 visits to their only daughter who lives in Hawaii. She is currently taking courses in poetry and philosophy at the University of California.

The grounds of her home are a refuge for stray animals of all kinds. Several years ago her book, *The Animal Convention,* was published. It is a story for children which tells of her concern for ecology. "I wrote it," says Barbara Jo, "so boys and girls would grow up knowing that some of my generation tried to stop the crimes being committed against our environment."

Barbara Jo lives quietly today in Santa Barbara, California. *(Jeannie Youngson)*

Ernestine Wade played Sapphire Stevens, wife of the Kingfish.

Alvin Childress had been on Broadway in *Anna Lucasta* and *Brown Sugar* before becoming Amos on television.

AMOS 'N' ANDY

The television version of the famed radio series debuted in 1951. By the time it went off the network in 1953 it was rated by viewers as either the funniest or the most offensive they had ever seen.

It was produced by Freeman F. Gosden and the late Charles Correll who had played the title roles on radio; they took great care with the casting.

Alvin Childress had a background of Broadway shows and films but he suspected he might not look right for any of the parts. So he spent months listening to air checks of the radio programs and mimicking all the voices. He was hired first in 1949 and spent a year helping to scout other actors. The role he won was Amos, owner of the Fresh Air Taxi Company (one cab) and father of Arbadella.

Ernestine Wade, who played the battleax Sapphire, had been on the radio show since 1939 playing Mrs. Henry Van Porter and the old maid Sara "Needlenose" Fletcher.

Spencer Williams who played Andy died in 1969, and Johnny Lee who was Lawyer Calhoon has been dead since 1965. The part of the slothful Lightnin', a character particularly criticized by civil rights groups, was taken by Nick Stuart. He now owns and operates the all-black Ebony Showcase Theatre in Los Angeles.